Principles of Programming:
an Introduction with Fortran

Principles of Programming:
an Introduction with Fortran

Edward B. James
Imperial College Computing Centre
London

PITMAN

PITMAN BOOKS LIMITED
39 Parker Street, London WC2B 5PB

Associated Companies
Pitman Publishing Pty Ltd, Melbourne
Pitman Publishing New Zealand Ltd, Wellington
Copp Clark Pitman, Toronto

© Edward B James 1978

First published in Great Britain 1978
Reprinted 1980 and 1981

All rights reserved. No part of this publication may be reproduced, stored in a retrieval system, or transmitted, in any form or by any means, electronic, mechanical, photocopying, recording and/or otherwise without the prior written permission of the publishers. This book may not be lent, resold, hired out or otherwise disposed of by way of trade in any form of binding or cover other than that in which it is published, without the prior consent of the publishers. This book is sold subject to the Standard Conditions of Sale of Net Books and may not be resold in the UK below the net price.

Printed and bound in Great Britain
at The Pitman Press, Bath

ISBN 0 273 01221 5

Preface

This book is designed to provide an introduction to programming for someone who has had no previous experience of computer use. We have provided an appreciation of how computers work and how to solve problems with the aid of a computer program. Then we have provided a description of significant features of the Fortran programming language coupled with examples to provide a good grounding in practical use. The amount of material and the method of presentation has been determined from experience in providing an introductory course for several thousands of students over the last thirteen years. These students have come from many different countries and have required to use computers in many different disciplines. We have not assumed any particular specialization and we have specifically excluded any mathematical requirement from text and examples. The amount of detail in the first eleven chapters has been determined by the requirement that they should be covered successfully in the equivalent of one week of full-time work. The final chapters provide an introduction to a professional style of programming and a critical survey of the complete Fortran language.

Throughout, the accent has been on the readability of the text. Although it has been developed in conjunction with a large-scale training course, it has also been used successfully by the individual students for a self-study course in preparation for later practical work. We hope it will provide a helpful guide into the computing world.

It is a pleasure to acknowledge the contribution of a great number of colleagues and students to the final form of this book. The original course text was developed in conjunction with Peter Whitehead and Fergus O'Brien and this latest text has been read and checked in detail by Roger Hunt, John Shelley and John Greenaway. Several student demonstrators have made valuable comments on the text, in particular Michael Poznanski.

Finally I would like to express my thanks to Eileen Armstrong for typing innumerable drafts and the final copy from which this book has been prepared.

Edward James
June 1978

A note for teachers

This book differs radically from other well-known texts in several respects.

First, it tries to present a coherent picture of the programming process which leads as smoothly as possible from problem solving to the preparation of the completed program. It introduces the concept of the *program plan* as a replacement for conventional flow charts and as the principal vehicle for ensuring the effective structuring and consequent understandability of the program which represents its lowest level of detail.

Second, it presents a *critical* coverage of the Fortran language. Where other texts strive to provide an exhaustive account of every feature in standard and even non-standard Fortran, we have chosen to describe a minimal subset of the 1966 standard which will guarantee the portability of the resulting programs to any computing centre. Clearly, it is not relevant to attempt to justify the exclusion of a considerable number of familiar features in an elementary text, but our simple omissions hopefully speak volumes on our experience of teaching and advising over many years.

Finally we have not provided a text from which the teacher can select certain parts and certain examples. In the first eleven chapters we have provided that which in our experience is exactly enough for the average non-specialist student to work on and master in the equivalent of a one-week course and we have purposely not provided extra material, because we know this only confuses the student. The contents have been determined in part from the analysis of hundreds of questionnaires returned by course attenders.

Teachers who are interested in details of the associated course structure and organisation are cordially invited to contact the author.

Contents

    Preface   v

1   Introduction to computing   1

    An appreciation of the component parts of a computer based on what we expect it to do.

2   Problem solving with a computing system   4

    The capabilities of the computer and how we start to sketch out the solution of a computing problem, with an example.

3   Refining the solution   7

    Putting more detail into a problem solution; sequences of instructions, decision-making and repetition; variable names and the storage of values. Planning a computer program.

4   The user interface   12

    Taking programs into the computer, translating them and making them work. Communication with the computer. The programming language, Fortran. Representing instructions and data.

5   Reading and writing   17

    Getting data into the computer and getting results out. The Fortran statements READ, WRITE and FORMAT. The building up for a complete program. The statements STOP and END.

6   Arithmetic   24

    How to specify numerical calculations. The Fortran assignment statement and its rules. The finiteness of computer arithmetic.

7   Program flow   29

    How to make decisions in programs. The Fortran logical IF, GO TO and CONTINUE statements. Programs as blocks of statements. Decisions and program loops.

8   Repetition with subscripted variables   36

    Processing data more than once. Storing collections of data. Arrays and subscripts. The Fortran DIMENSION statement.

9   The control of repetition   40

    Simplifying the control of repetition. The Fortran DO statement
    and rules for use.

10 Structuring the program: subprograms and parameters   44

    Problems with large programs and the need for dividing up.
    Subprograms and how they are represented. The Fortran SUBROUTINE,
    RETURN and CALL statements. Communication between subprograms
    and parameters.

11 Additional features   50

    Extensions to the previous statements and some useful additions.
    The Fortran COMMON statement, the FORMAT statement and the layout
    of results. The implied DO loop. Logical expressions in the
    logical IF statement. Library functions.

12 Programming quality   58

    The idea of quality in programming. The programming process and
    the management of resources. A program design method and the
    program plan. Program qualities and techniques for promoting
    them. The importance of a standard language.

13 A survey of FORTRAN   65

    A critical survey of Fortran statements and recommendations on
    their use. Data objects, the storage of data, calculation and
    assignment, input and output, program flow, program structure.
    On not using special features.

14 Further progress   78

    Gaining experience in programming. Practical work, software
    tools and program management, with recommended further reading.
    Programming in the future.

    Solutions to exercises   80

    Appendix 1   Control statements   89

    Appendix 2   Number representation   91

    Index   92

1 Introduction to computing

The computer is a tool that helps people to deal with problems. It is assumed that the reader wants to find out about computing because there is a possibility that it may be useful in the future. In fact, computing can help us in such a wide range of activities that it is necessary to focus on certain particular ones in order to get started.

The first computers were used for performing rather complicated mathematical calculations which could not be done quickly enough by hand, and this has remained an important role for the computer. Since those times, the range of activities which can be carried out has expanded beyond recognition to every field of human action, but the basic structure of the computers themselves (for better or worse) has hardly changed and it is still most convenient to introduce the technique of computing through the carrying out of simple numerical calculations. This is true both for those who wish to proceed to large-scale numerical work and for those who will later work in fields described as non-numeric; for example, in commercial data-processing, in picture-processing, or in the linguistic analysis of literary texts.

Most readers will have heard already about computer programs, which are the means of defining what the computer is to do, and so it would seem reasonable to get on straight away with learning how to construct these programs. The aim of much recent work by computing specialists is to make it possible for ordinary people to get things done on computers without the need to be involved with complicated details of computer operation. Sadly, we are still very far from this ideal state, and in the meantime it is very valuable to have some appreciation of the way computers work, if only in outline, so that we can appreciate what is sensible to do and what is not sensible to expect. A very small amount of experience in this area will be very helpful in countering the rather strange ideas about computing which circulate in the community, often as a result of the activities of the popular press. So let us build up an idea of how computers work from an analysis of what they are supposed to do for us.

About computers

Let us consider how a computer can be made to perform some calculations. It is helpful here to think of the situation when a colleague has offered to help us with some tedious arithmetic. What do we have to provide for this useful person to enable him to assist in the calculations?

First, we must tell him what needs to be done. In more detail, we must provide a set of *instructions* to tell him how to achieve the results that we want. Then, he must be provided with some *data* to work on. This could be, for example, a collection of numbers which must be added together. It is just the same with a computer. The computer requires some instructions and some data before it can calculate results. Now we can consider how the computer is arranged internally.

Since it requires instructions and data then there must be some way of introducing them. We can think of both the instructions and data as being in written form and so we require some form of *input* device which takes in such material and converts it into a form suitable for the computer to work with. At the present time, electronics provides us with the most convenient technology for constructing computers, and so the information in the instructions and data is coded into suitable electrical signals. We may represent this diagramatically as follows:

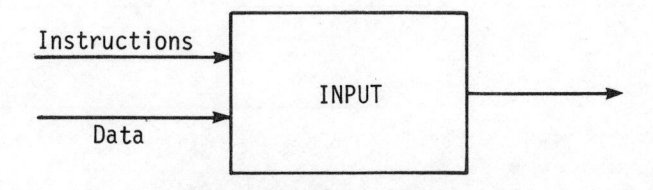

What happens after this? Most people would assume that since the objective is to carry out calculations, then these should be set in motion straight away. In fact, a consideration of the *order* in which things must happen will make it clear that we cannot start calculating immediately. In the case of a helpful colleague, he must first get clear in his mind what is to be done *before* he can get to work on the data. So the instructions must be first stored in his *memory*.

In exactly the same way, the instructions given to the computer must be stored away in something corresponding to a memory before it can start to take in the data. This section of the computer which remembers things is called the *store*. Again if we think of thousands of items of data being processed it is clear that they must be organized into some sort of order and since they cannot be all processed at once, there must be storage space for at least some of them inside the computer while they wait for the previous data to be processed. In the same way, all the results cannot be printed out at once and so the results must also be stored in the computer until it is time to print them out through some sort of *output* unit. We begin to see then, that computer operations are mainly focused on the store, because that is where most operations begin and end. Even the arithmetic is done by taking numbers from the store, performing calculations and putting the answers back into the store. So we can sketch in more detail as follows:

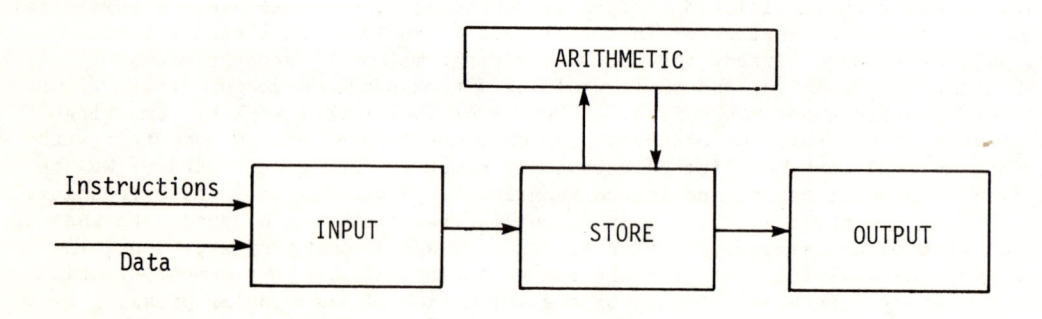

```
                          ┌─────────────┐
                          │  ARITHMETIC │
                          └──────┬──────┘
                                 ↕
Instructions ──┐   ┌───────┐   ┌─────┐   ┌────────┐
               ├──→│ INPUT │──→│STORE│──→│ OUTPUT │
Data       ────┘   └───────┘   └─────┘   └────────┘
```

This seems to take care of the flow of data inside the computer. But what about the instructions? In fact they are taken into a part of the store separate from the data and then taken out one by one to be interpreted by a *control* unit. This determines what the instruction requires to have done and sends electronic signals to each of the other boxes to carry out the required operation. We can represent this control by dotted lines.

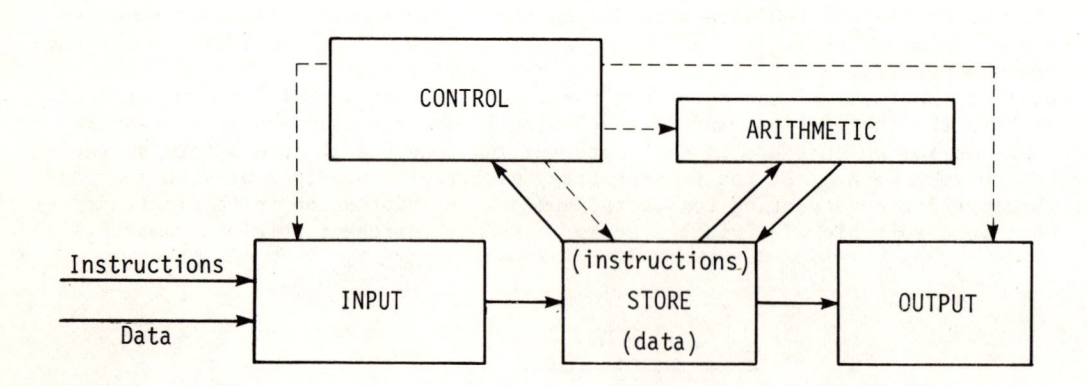

```
                 ┌─────────┐         ┌────────────┐
                 │ CONTROL │ ──────→ │ ARITHMETIC │
                 └─────────┘         └────────────┘
                                          
Instructions ──┐   ┌───────┐   ┌──────────────┐   ┌────────┐
               ├──→│ INPUT │──→│ (instructions)│──→│ OUTPUT │
Data       ────┘   └───────┘   │    STORE     │   └────────┘
                               │    (data)    │
                               └──────────────┘
```

It will be seen that the store occupies the critical position in all the operations and has to act very quickly. Since speed costs money, we cannot afford to store all the information we would like in the so-called immediate access store. So we have to provide slower

2

(and therefore cheaper) forms of *auxiliary* storage which can feed in information to the central store when required.

Another complication arises from the imbalance between the very fast, electronic central store and arithmetic unit and the much slower mechanical input and output units. A normal large computer has many different input and output units connected to it, and since the central part is so fast it can keep a large number of users of the various input and output units happy by sharing its time between them, providing a *timesharing* service.

As there are many different ways of presenting data to the computer, there is a great variety of input units. Earlier methods include representing each letter or number as a series of holes on *punched cards* or on continuous *paper tape*. More recent developments allow the user to provide information via a typewriter-like *keyboard* connected directly with the computer. Printed data of good quality can be read directly off the page and it is becoming possible to provide certain simple types of input directly from the spoken word. The traditional printed output has in many cases been replaced by television-like *visual display* units and it is possible to obtain complex pictures as well as the conventional words and numbers at full size, or in reduced size on *microfilm*.

The collection of mechanical and electronic components which together constitute the computer is known in the jargon as the *hardware* and here is a final complete diagram.

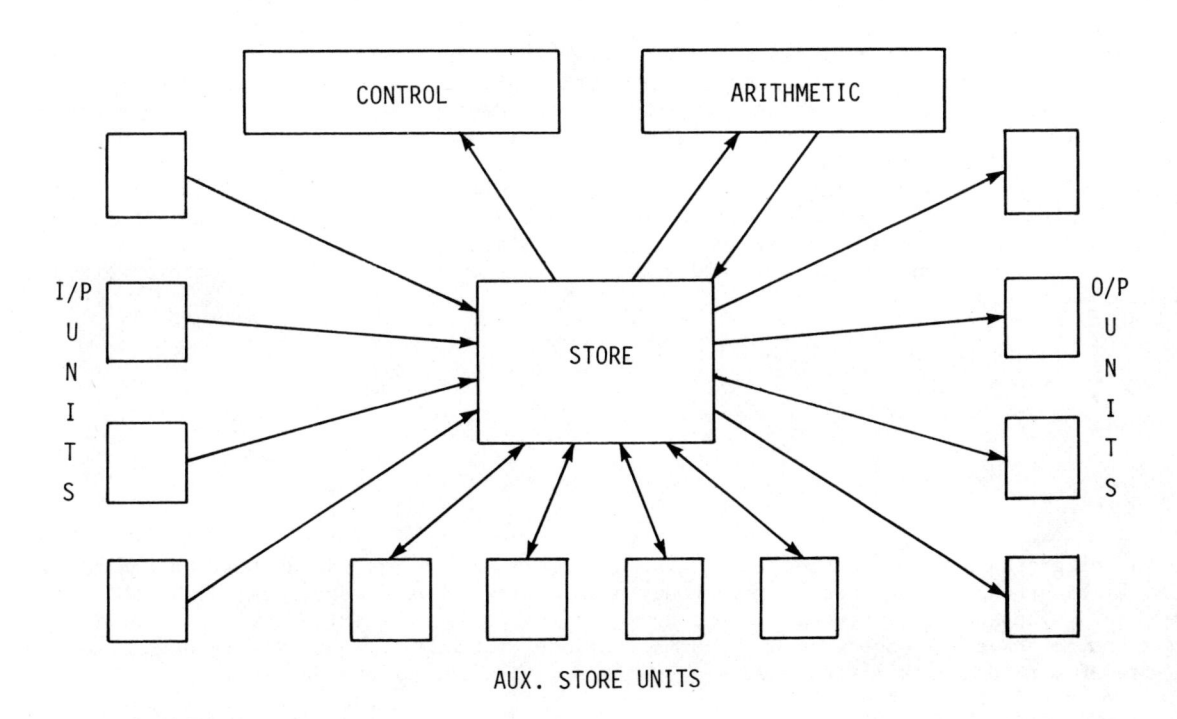

Notice that *every* computer from the smallest to the largest operates in exactly the same way; the only difference is in the multiplicity of the units which are connected together.

About programming

The computer we have just described is very general in its purpose. It can take in many different sorts of data and process them in a wide variety of different ways to produce results, according to the instructions provided. We can view the computer as a general-purpose machine which is turned into a special-purpose machine to do exactly the job we currently require by means of a particular set of instructions which we call a *program*.

The difference between being assisted with calculations by a helpful colleague and by a computer lies in the very great difference in the detail of the instructions which these two assistants require. Instructions to a colleague can be very general and there are many things which he will already know about. But at the present time a computer requires an incredibly detailed sequence of instructions to perform the simplest of tasks. Preparing the program can take so much effort that only the processing of a very great amount of data or the use of the same program on many different occasions can possibly justify the effort involved. We now turn to study the programming process, starting with the analysis of the problem to be solved with computer assistance and leading to the preparation of a suitable program.

2 Problem solving with a computing system

The reader will soon discover that there is much more to using computers effectively than writing down sequences of instructions. The final writing down of the program in a language which can be acted on by a particular computer is a relatively straightforward part of programming. Before this must come the determination of what the particular problem *is* and how the computer can be involved in the solution. Now we move into a difficult area because no one knows how someone else solves a problem. It is a question of weighing up what is required, and what resources are available to assist the solution, and then deciding how to employ them. The experienced person can only provide some general principles for guidance and demonstrate the solution of some particular problems. Then the intelligence of the learner comes into play and fills in the gap between problem and solution in any particular instance.

Let us consider the capabilities of the computer as an assistant. It can take in some data and store it away. It can take data from its store and send it back into the outside world. And finally, it can combine data together arithmetically and in other ways to produce new values. It is amazing how useful these simple abilities can be. Let us consider a particular problem and demonstrate a solution to it. The problem chosen may seem trivially simple, but surprisingly the solution involves most of the activities which will later be employed to build up solutions to the largest of problems. It is simply this: given a collection of numbers in any order, find the biggest one.

It is worth first considering how this would be done 'by hand'. If the numbers were written down on a page, for example:

2
12
93
186
42
81
17

then the biggest one could be seen "at a glance", for it would extend furthest to the left. It should be stressed that there is never any possibility of using short cuts like this in computing. The subtle ways in which the human eye and brain can extract information from such a 'scene' have no connection with normal computer methods. So if we are unable to make use of such human skills to devise a computer method then where do we start? At this point the very limitations of the computer come to our aid. It can do so few different things, that it becomes merely a question of considering a suitable sequence of these. So let us try a few possibilities. What do we do first?

In fact we start by looking at the data and its arrangement (and this will be true of every problem in the future). It is probably simplest to imagine that the sequence of numbers in which we are looking for the biggest is arranged with one number on each of a collection of punched cards. The program is always written assuming that the data is *outside* the computer waiting to come in; no computing can be done without *some* data to work on. So the first thing we need to think of is getting data into store. Let us feed in (the technical term is *read in*) one of the data numbers. Which one? Here we find the physical constraints of early computers have led to a fixed way of specifying the reading in of data. If data is provided in the form of punched cards, it is practically possible to read them into the computer only in the order in which they are stacked. So a command to "read in" can only obtain the *next* piece of information from the stack of cards. This idea has become built into the computing process even if we do not use punched cards; so 'READ' always implies "Read in the *next* item of data of a fixed sequence".

Now is the time to think of the problem. It is to find the *biggest* number, and so has to do with *comparing* numbers for size. We cannot do much comparing of numbers with only one of them in the machine, so we have to take another number in. What next?

Here again, a second fundamental principle comes to our aid. Storing data in computers costs storage space, so it is as well to have as little inside as possible at any one time. Therefore, the principle is to start computation as soon as there is sufficient data in the computer to work on. Since there are already two numbers in the computer, they can be compared, and we can forget about the smaller one, since it will obviously not be involved in further decision about the biggest of all. So the smaller is discarded, leaving the bigger as still of interest. What next?

Well, we have returned to having only one interesting piece of data inside the computer. To compute, we require two, and therefore there is nothing to do but to take in the next data number. Now the second principle just mentioned asks for some computation, and the obvious thing to do is to compare the number which has just come in with the one left from the previous operation. Again, the smaller of these can be discarded, and we are left with the biggest number encountered so far.

At this stage, we shall begin to see a pattern in the sequence of operations, which will lead to the required answer if it is repeated a sufficient number of times. The process to be repeated is

> *Read in the next value*
> *Compare it with the one already in the computer*
> *Keep the bigger of the two*

If this is repeated *until* there are no more values to be taken in, we shall be left with a single number, the largest, inside the machine. It is then necessary only to print it out to provide the answer.

The fact that a solution has been arrived at so quickly with apparently little choice of what to do on the way may lead us to believe that computing can assist with only a very limited range of problems. In fact, very slight adjustments in the nature of the computation which we perform, as the data is taken in bit by bit, will be able to produce a very great variety of results. The other remarkable thing is how soon it was possible to spot the sequence that was required to be repeated to produce the result. We shall discover that if this repetition cannot be established rather easily, then there will be no point in using a computer. If we cannot say "repeat this sequence for each data value" then the number of instructions is going to be about the same as the number of pieces of data and it will be just as fast to process each number by hand as to write down the corresponding instruction. Notice that it is never a question of an *exact* repetition. The *same* operation is done each time to a *different* piece of data and so the result will differ at each repetition.

Now let us consider how to write down our solution. At this stage of the work, it is natural to write down our ideas in a rough note form and in the language in which we are accustomed to think. Essentially, we are creating a *sequence* of instructions and these can each be written down on a separate line in the order in which they will be carried out. So the first few instructions in the present example may look like

> *Read in the first number*
> *Read in the second number*
> *Compare the first and second numbers*
> *Keep the bigger of these two*

A problem arises as soon as we get to that part of the instructions which is to be repeated. We need to be able to refer to the block of instructions to be repeated as a single entity and to say "repeat this block until ....". It will be natural to separate off the instructions which are to be repeated, say with an enclosing bracket, and write next to it the condition which decides when to stop the repetition. After the repetition stops we can continue to write down instructions in sequence as before.

As soon as we try to do this with the present example another problem occurs. The part which requires repetition is clearly

> [*Read in the second number*
> *Compare the first and second numbers*
> *Keep the bigger of these two*

But it was written down while we were still thinking of specific numbers, the first and second, and it is only after doing this that we see that the situation can be *generalized* and repeated in the form

> [*Read in the next number*
> *Compare it with the one remaining in the computer*
> *Keep the bigger of these two*

The generalization is not concerned with the operations but with the names of the things we are operating on and this will always be true. We start by thinking of particular values of data and what needs to be done to them, and then generalize the situation and describe what needs to be done in terms of names which can refer to a *variable* value of the data. Later on we shall encounter rules for constructing these names in a particular programming language, but for now we can use any convenient word, preferably one which reminds us of what the corresponding value represents or *means*. The repeating part can be written as

> *Read in the next number and call it NEW*
> *Compare it with the one remaining, OLD*
> *Keep the bigger of these two and call it OLD*

However, on returning to the first instruction of all, we see that the natural way of putting it

> *Read in the next number and call it FIRST*

is incompatible with the two names *NEW* and *OLD* which occur in the repeated part. If we look at the repeated part, we shall see that the value which started off as first number in has become generalized to the number which has remained in the computer because it is the *biggest* so far, that is, *OLD*. In programming there is always this tension between what happens at the start of a program and what happens once the essential repetitive pattern has been established. In this particular example we can resolve the problem of names by writing

> *Read in the next (first) number and call it OLD*

and then the repeated part can follow on consistently. After the repetitions have finished, that is, all the input values have been processed, the result can be written out.

Putting all these ideas together, we can construct a first draft of our solution as follows:

> *Read in the first number and call it OLD*
>
> *Read in the next number and call it NEW*
> *Compare NEW with OLD*
> *Keep the larger and call it OLD*
>
> *Repeat the previous three instructions until there*
> *are no more data values to process*
> *Print out OLD which will be the largest of all the numbers*
> *Stop*

In later versions of the *plan* it may seem more natural to put the conditions for repetition before the bracket rather than after.

The most important thing to notice about this initial phase of problem solving is that it is a messy process requiring several false starts and alterations as we progress towards the solution. This is of the essence of creative work. Now it will be useful to have some practice in applying these principles to a few other problems before looking at the programming process in greater detail.

Examples

Prepare outline solutions in rough note form as demonstrated in the text to perform the following tasks:

2.1 Find the sum of a collection of positive numbers.

2.2 There are M numbers in a list of positive numbers. Count how many of them are greater than a given value (VALUE).

2.3 Sort a list of N positive numbers into descending order of value.
    (This example is much more difficult and is probably best studied by referring to the solution at the back of the book.)

3 Refining the solution

It is an unfortunate fact that while a helpful friend might be able to assist us if provided with one of the outline solutions we have devised in the previous chapter, such a solution cannot be presented to a computer until much more work has been done on it. What the computer requires is a *program*, a detailed sequence of statements in a particular programming language which can be interpreted directly into the mechanical and electronic activities necessary to produce the required result. So we must take our outline solution and add more detail until each requirement can be related directly to one or more statements in a particular programming language. Unfortunately, this is not an easy process to explain because somewhere along the way we shall be involved in a change in our method of *representing* the solution. The change has to occur because people do not naturally think about solving problems in terms of the operations which a computer has to perform in order to produce the results. Before we can discuss this further however, we must describe some of the operations which the computer can be asked to perform and show how they can be related to an outline solution.

As we stressed in the first chapter, most computer operations begin and end in the store and we must now consider the structure of the store in greater detail. It is helpful to view it as a large collection of *boxes*, each of which can hold a useful number or *value*. Each box will be associated with a *name* which enables us to refer to the value contained in it. We can now identify these names with the names used previously in the outline solutions and the corresponding boxes will be used to hold the numbers we are talking about.

When a number is read into the computer, a box must be provided in the store to hold it. So the instruction "Read in the next number and call it NEW" means "Read in the next number and put it in the storage box *called* NEW". Although it is a good thing to use box names which describe the purpose of the number in the box, for the present we will emphasize that we are talking about boxes by giving them neutral names such as A, B and C. The long instruction "Read the next number in and put it in a box called B" can be shortened to "Read into B".

The output operation involves a storage box in a similar way. In this case the number to be printed out must be ready in a storage box and the printing instruction must refer to the name of that storage box. The instruction "Print out from A" will mean "Take the number from the storage box called A and print it out".

Referring to the outline solution obtained in the previous chapter we can put it in more precise terms as

   Read into B

  [*Read into A*
   Compare A with B
   Keep the larger and call it B

   Repeat the previous three instructions until all the data values have been processed
   Print out from B
   Stop

The next consideration is to replace the rather vague phrases such as 'Keep the larger' and 'until there are no more data values' with more precise instructions related to storage boxes.

The first vague phrase is "Compare A with B". This is actually connected very closely with the following instruction and we will have to consider both together in order to relate them to computer processes. Here, for the first time, we are involved in a *decision process*: if the new contents of A (the value just read in) are actually greater than the contents of B (which is holding the greatest so far) then we want to retain the contents of A. Otherwise, we want to retain the contents of B and ignore the contents of A. This can be written concisely as follows:

   If A is greater than B
   then replace B with A
   otherwise do nothing

There are several basic computing principles hidden under these instructions. The phrase following "If" asks for a decision. The answer to the implied question: "Is A greater than B" can be answered "yes" or "no" depending on the present values of A and B. If the answer is "yes" then we need to do what is requested after the word "then" in the instruction sequence. If the answer is "no" then we need to do what is asked for after the word "otherwise", in this case, nothing. So the answer to the question is used to decide between two courses of action. Only one of these is carried out, according to the answer to the question. If the two alternative courses of action are quite lengthy in themselves it may be useful to lay them out as follows:

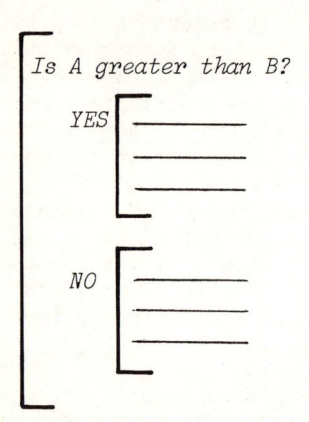

[
Is A greater than B?

YES [─────
      ─────
      ─────

NO [─────
      ─────
      ─────
]

The question mark indicates a decision and the two blocks of instruction following it indicate what to do next according to whether the answer to the question is YES or NO.

After the YES *or* NO block has been performed we will return to the normal sequence of instructions which will naturally be written down to follow the decision process. The solution to the whole problem can be written down as follows:

[
Read into B
Read into A
   [*Is A greater than B?*
     YES [*Replace B with A*
     NO [*Go on to next instruction*
   ]

Repeat these instructions until all the data values have been processed
Print out from B
Stop
]

For consistency we have put an enclosing bracket round the complete plan, indicating that all the enclosed components are part of the complete solution.

Another important programming principle is concerned with what happens to the value in a box when it is referred to by another instruction. This depends on what the second instruction says. If the second instruction is putting a new value in the box (such as "Read into A") then the old value which was previously in A will be *totally* destroyed as the new value takes its place. Notice that a small number like 2 can totally replace a large number like 36,548,928 because all numbers in the computer are represented in a way which will completely fill a box; so 2 is represented as 00000002 with as many zeros as are required to fill a box. However, if we ask for a *transfer* of the value from a box which has been filled with a number previously, such as in the instruction "Replace B with A" where the value in A is to be transferred into the box B, then we will end up with the same value in *both* boxes. This is because 'transfer from A' is realised by taking a *copy* of the value in A and putting it into B. The original value in A remains but of course the old value in B is completely destroyed. We can therefore 'transfer from A' as many times as we like without destroying its contents. This apparently unbalanced behaviour is derived from the way in which the electronics, which is used to realize the storage boxes, most naturally works.

The convention just described can be illustrated by going through the movements of data suggested by our solution to the present problem.

In the first instruction the first data value is taken into the computer and placed in the box called B. The first instruction in the repetitive sequence places the second and successive data values into the box called A. There is a comparison between the values in B and A and if A is greater, then a *copy* of the value in A is transferred into B. Notice at this stage that A and B have the same value in them. Otherwise, if A is *not* greater, then B retains its original value. At this stage the value in A is not significant because when "Read into A" is repeated, whatever was there is overwritten by the next data value coming in. To get the operations clear, it is useful to write some sample data values on a collection of cards and go through the operations by hand exactly as specified. This *simulation* of the computing process will prove very valuable in testing programs for correctness later.

Now let us refine the instruction which controls the repetitive sequence. How do we decide in detail when there are no more data numbers left to process?

If we knew exactly how many data values were to be processed then we could request the repetition a specific number of times. But remembering that a program is only valuable as far as it can be used more than once, it is clearly best to write a program which can process any number of data values at a particular time. This is most easily done by putting at the end of the data values a special marker which effectively stops the repetitions and leads to the printing out of the result. Now this marker must be read in just like any of the data values because the computer cannot be instructed to check that it *is* the marker until it is in a storage box. This leads to a rather strange requirement in the instructions, that *every* value read in must be checked to see if it is the end marker. So clearly there needs to be another decision process in the instructions. As soon as "Read into A" is completed, we need to decide whether A contains a data value or the end marker. For simplicity let us use as an end marker a number which does not occur as a data value, say 999, for the values we wish to process in this program.

The decision process can be written down as follows:

```
Read into A
   ⎡ Is A equal to 999?
   ⎢    YES ⎡ Stop the repetition and continue
   ⎢        ⎣ with the following instructions
   ⎢
   ⎣    NO  ⎡ Do the rest of the repetition (that is, process the
            ⎣ value in A knowing it is not the end marker)
```

'Stopping the repetition' involves getting out of the repeating part of the process completely and going on to the sequence following the repetition. It seems natural to use a word like EXIT in this position which will imply that the next thing to be done is written following the repetition bracket and after any instructions concerning the repetition.

In this particular example the NO part of the decision involves all the significant work in the repetition. After the NO instructions are carried out we will require to repeat the whole process again from "Read into A" and it is natural to use the word REPEAT to indicate this just below the collection of 'NO' instructions. So the whole process can be described as follows:

```
⎡ Read into B
⎢   ⎡ Read into A
⎢   ⎢   ⎡ Is A equal to 999?
⎢   ⎢   ⎢     YES ⎡ EXIT
⎢   ⎢   ⎢
⎢   ⎢   ⎣     NO  ⎡ Is A greater than B?
⎢   ⎢             ⎢    YES ⎡ Replace B with A
⎢   ⎢             ⎣    NO  ⎡ Go on to next instruction
⎢   ⎣ Repeat
⎢ Printout from B
⎣ Stop
```

In this particular example the bottom of four brackets happens to coincide and "Go on to next instruction" is in a sense the last thing to be done in all four of them. The REPEAT instruction is written below the longest bracket of the four to indicate that repetition occurs after the last instruction in *that* bracket (which is actually the last instruction in the following bracket (which is actually the last instruction in the following bracket (which is actually the last instruction in the following bracket, that is "Go on to next instruction")))! This idea of brackets inside brackets inside brackets that is, of hierarchies of control, is fundamental to computing. Notice that when the repetition occurs we start again at the top of the bracket against which REPEAT is written.

We have refined the solution and provided enough detail as is necessary before the process of *coding*, that is writing the solution in a particular programming language. Now we can look at the total problem-solving process as already described by means of a particular example and present it in an organised way.

Referring back to the previous chapter, we started with two 'givens': a knowledge of the required output (the 'biggest' number) and a knowledge of the information available as input (a collection of numbers). From these two, by analogy and experience, we constructed the process which is required to convert the input into the output. In more difficult problems the data input and the required output will have more complicated structures. The input data may have to be checked for consistency or arranged in a different order for processing. The output results may have to be displayed in columns or rows with suitable headings, or sorted into a different order to that in which they were computed. So any computing process tends to have three parts: a beginning section carried out once; a main processing section repeated many times; and finally a closing section carried out once only. The planning diagram will represent it as

$$\left[\begin{array}{l} \textit{BEGINNING SECTION (once)} \\ \textit{MAIN SECTION (many times)} \\ \textit{CLOSING SECTION (once)} \end{array}\right.$$

How many times the *main section* is repeated will normally depend on some property of the input data, such as how many items of data are to be processed and so any repetitive process will be controlled by a YES-NO decision process or sequence of such processes.

When we start to refine the solution, that is to put more detail into the sections already specified, we shall discover a strange thing. Each of the already existing sections may be broken down in turn just as the total problem is, and this can be repeated until we get down towards the programming language level of detail. In fact, in some special types of problem this process of step-by-step refinement can appear to be continued right down to the programming language level. But due to the difference referred to previously between the way we break the problem down in our mind and the way the computer eventually builds up the results, this is not a *clean* process. However, the more the program as it is written down can be easily related to conceptual sub-sections in the problem solving process, the easier we will remember how it works and be able to explain it to other people. We shall discover later that such conveniences are fundamental to successful programming.

The method of sketching problem solutions presented here will be referred to later as a program *plan*. It is not intended that the reader should copy the method slavishly. All that is being suggested is that brackets can be used to separate off individual parts of the problem solution in the early stages and later they can be used in conjunction with words like YES, NO, EXIT and REPEAT to clarify decision processes and repetition.

It is very tempting to formalize the method and complicate the planning language until the specification of the solution is so detailed as to be in competition and even in conflict with the eventual program as a means of describing the detailed computing process. Problem solving is very much a personal task and the methods used to describe a solution in the early stages of development may be expected to be special to an individual. However, if the program is going to be useful for a long time and to be useful to other people, it should be possible for someone else to recreate the program in a different programming language from what the original programmer has left behind.

Examples

3.1 Re-write the solutions to the examples on page 6 providing more details in a program plan as described in this chapter. Assume that each number to be processed is punched on a card and that the last number in the list is followed by a card with the special value -999.

3.2 Consider how each of the solutions will be changed if negative values are allowed in the lists.

3.3 A set of cards comprises a number of separate lists of positive numbers, all these values being punched one per card. Each separate list is followed by a card having the value -1.0 on it, except for the last list which is followed by a card with the value -2.0 on it. Prepare a program plan to find the *first* list which contains the greatest value contained amongst all the lists.
(This is intended as a more testing example and need not be completed before proceeding to the next exercise.)

4 The user interface

We have described the component parts of a computer and how to plan a computer program. It would be very pleasant if the computer could be given the program plan and so produce the solution without further effort on our part. Unfortunately, computer systems are not yet sophisticated enough to do this, and we must first convert our program plan into a sequence of instructions written in a particular *programming language* before it can be presented to the computer. This sequence of instructions is the computer *program*. The programming language we shall be describing is called *Fortran*, which was one of the first computer languages and is still very widely used.

The operating system

We have now to consider how the program which is created as a sequence of instructions outside the computer can be taken inside and made to work. Strangely enough, it requires only a slight change in perspective to relate this to a process already covered in some detail. Imagine that a certain program is already at work inside the computer. It will require some input *data*. Let us define this input data as the *program* which we wish to get into the computer. What is this first program to do? Its job is to get the second program into operation. Now we must consider something more about computer operation.

We have seen that activities in the computer are initiated by instructions taken in sequence from the storage of the computer and sent to the *control unit* which interprets them and sends the necessary control signals to make them happen to the other relevant parts of the machine. The control unit is able to interpret only instructions written in *machine code* which is a primitive language directly related to operations in the electronics of a particular computer. So the first program must be written in this machine code. Its first job will be to take in the second program and place it in storage. But this second program will be written in a programming language suitable for a computer user such as Fortran. It will not be written in machine code. Before it can be set into operation to produce results it must be *translated* into machine code. So the first program, already written in machine code, must carry out this translation as well. Then the second program can be set into operation to deal with the reading in of its own data. It is useful at this stage to consider the operations of the computer as it deals with several different users' programs in succession. We can sketch the operations as follows:

> *Take in user's program*
>
> *Translate from Fortran language into machine code*
>
> *Set resulting machine code program into operation*
>
> *Repeat while any users' programs remain outside*

The process of translation is usually called *compilation*. When a program is in operation producing results, the process is usually called *execution*. The special program which carries out the operations we have sketched is called an *operating system*. Its job is to supervise all the users' programs and get them into operation. So in some sense it is in operation all the time, handing over control temporarily to each user's program as it goes into execution, and then taking over again to process the next user's program. Apart from translation, it performs a variety of administrative jobs as well. Exactly what these are depends on a particular user's requirements, and so in addition to the program itself, the user has to provide information to help the operating system. The form in which this information is to be provided varies with different computers, but the nature of the information is naturally the same.

First, there must be some evidence that the following program comes from someone authorized to make use of the computer facilities. This is generally proved by quoting a 'user number'. Then there needs to be some indication of the computing resources required to enable the program to be executed, since this will enable the totality of resources to be scheduled efficiently. For example, a program requiring a lot of calculation but little printing of output might be executed at nearly the same time as a program with little calculation but a great deal of printing.

The next piece of information concerns the translating or compiling process. User programs may be written in a wide variety of different 'user languages' of which Fortran is only one. Clearly the computer must be told which of these has to be translated into machine code. In more complex programs there may be many other items to specify, such as the whereabouts in the computer's auxiliary storage of certain files of information to be used in conjunction with the present program.

If the program is presented through the medium of punched cards, then all this initial operating information will be on a series of punched cards preceding the program proper. It is then necessary to have a special card to mark the division between the initial sequence, often called 'control cards' and the program proper. A similar marker card will usually be necessary between the program and the user's data values, and finally there is a card which marks the end of the complete sequence belonging to a particular user. Following this will be another complete sequence or 'deck' as it is usually called, belonging to another user and so on. If the program is typed directly into the computer, there will be a corresponding sequence of 'operating instructions', program and data records with separation indicators between them. The 'control cards' relevant to the local computer are specified in appendix 1.

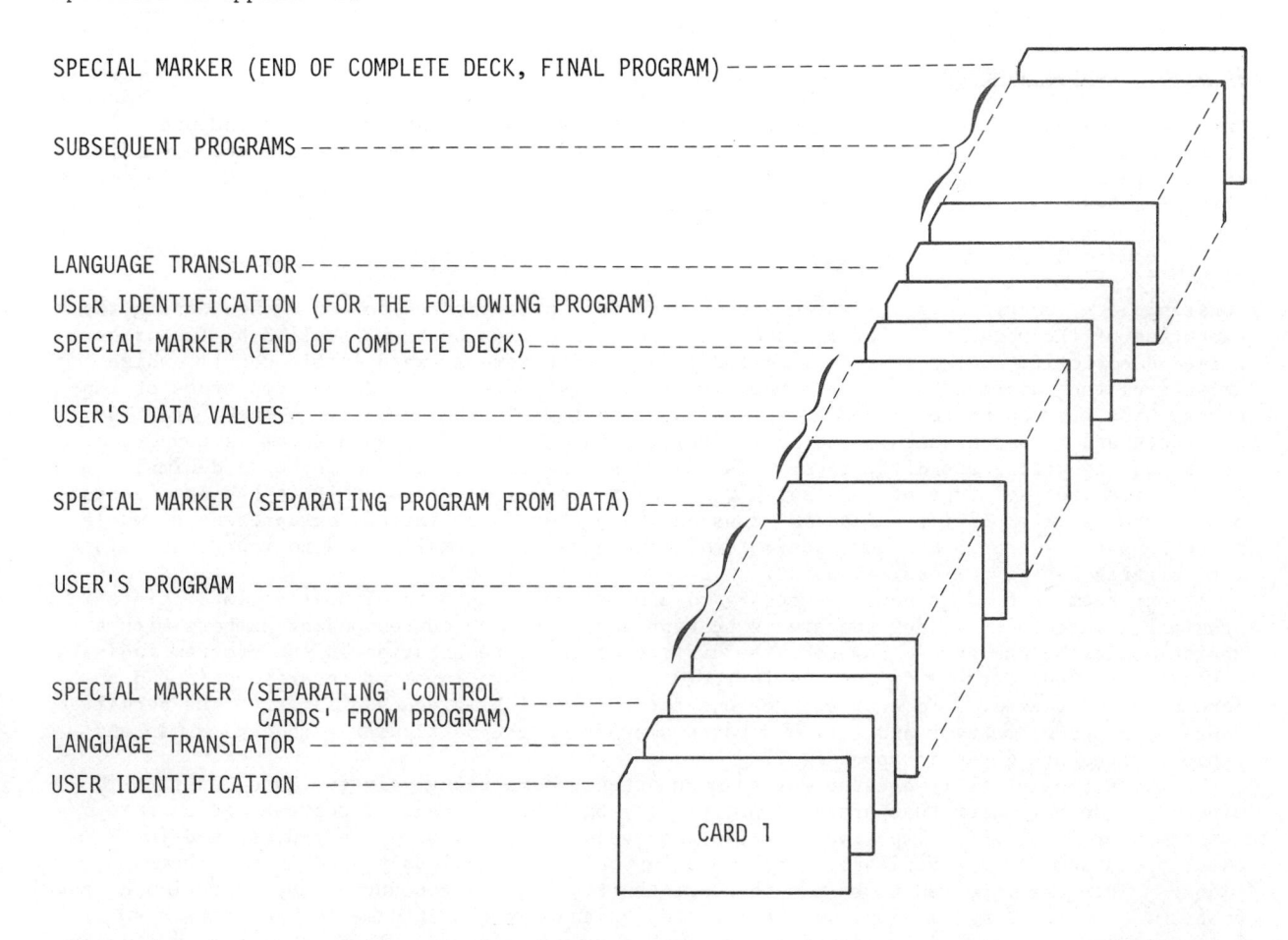

SPECIAL MARKER (END OF COMPLETE DECK, FINAL PROGRAM) ----------------

SUBSEQUENT PROGRAMS -----------------------------

LANGUAGE TRANSLATOR ---------------------------
USER IDENTIFICATION (FOR THE FOLLOWING PROGRAM) -----------
SPECIAL MARKER (END OF COMPLETE DECK) -----------------

USER'S DATA VALUES ---------------------------

SPECIAL MARKER (SEPARATING PROGRAM FROM DATA) ------

USER'S PROGRAM --------------------------

SPECIAL MARKER (SEPARATING 'CONTROL
              CARDS' FROM PROGRAM) -------
LANGUAGE TRANSLATOR -----------------
USER IDENTIFICATION ----------------

CARD 1

In most large computer installations, the operating program which processes all the users' programs is more a collection of related programs which call each other into operation as required and are known in toto as the *operating system*. Obvious components are programs for the translation from each of a range of user languages into machine code and each of these is called a *compiler*.

The user's total requirements are communicated to the computer through the information contained in the operating instructions and in the user's program. The user receives information from the computer in the form of results together with other messages initiated by the operating system as it attempts to obey the user's instructions. This totality of messages forms the link between user and computer and is usually called the *user interface*.

13

Communications with the computer

We are now concerned with the way in which users present their requirements to the computer and the form in which results are returned. In both cases we are concerned with messages and these are usually in written form. Written messages require a collection of different symbols to transmit them and in computing these are called *characters*. The set of acceptable characters depends on which computer and which programming language is in use. The set available to most users of the Fortran language is as follows:

    The Capital Letters A-Z
    The numbers   0-9
    Special Characters: +(plus) -(minus or hyphen) *(asterisk) /(slash) =(equals)
    () (open and closed brackets) .(full stop or decimal point) ,(comma) '(quote)
    £ or $ (currency sign)

and so this is the collection we shall use to construct statements in the programming language. It is also the set of characters which can be used to print out the results. So everything in programming with the Fortran language will be done by using these characters.

Data and program components

Until now, we have been describing general characteristics of programming and computer operation. Now we can get down to the details of coding a problem solution into a particular programming language, Fortran. It is useful first to consider two elementary components which are used in a variety of different program statements

> *constants* and *variables*

Constants are numerical values which are written into programs and do not change during the execution of the program. For instance, something requires to be multiplied by two or have three added to it. Here we are immediately faced with some awkward little details which arise from the nature of computers themselves. It is necessary to define two types of constant which correspond to different ways of storing them in the computer. These are *integer* constants and *real* constants. As far as writing them into a Fortran program is concerned, it is easy to define the difference. The *integer* type of constant *never* has a decimal point while the *real* type of constant *always* has a decimal point (even if it has no figures behind the decimal point). *Integer* constants are therefore limited to representing whole numbers up to a certain maximum size. *Real* constants are normally used to represent values with figures behind the decimal point.

It may seem that it is never necessary to use *integer* constants without decimal points in programs, since their values can always be represented by the corresponding numbers with a decimal point on the end. However, the difference in representation in the program indicates a very considerable difference in their behaviour when involved in arithmetic and so both have to be used. Some of the reasons for this will be discussed later. The permitted range of sizes of integer and real constants depends on the particular computer in use and typical sizes are given in appendix 2.

It may not be clear at present why so much attention is being paid to these constants, since they do not occur that often in programs. But their method of representation *inside* the computer is of great importance because the values of *variables* are represented in exactly the same way. Variables correspond to the names previously used in the program plans. They are referred to by *name* because their *value* changes during the execution of the program. In the program plans we are free to use any convenient name to represent a value, but when they are used in Fortran they are much more restricted. In Fortran they naturally must use characters which can be represented in the machine, and each name is between one and six characters; the first one must be a letter of the alphabet (A-Z) and the others can be a letter of the alphabet or a digit (0-9). So possible variable names are, for example:

    A   B3   LENGTH   WIDTH   SIZE2

Notice that full stops or commas or brackets or similar characters are *not* permitted.

Since the values corresponding to these variable names have to be represented in the storage space of the computer, the problem of integer and real values is with us again. It is necessary to arrange for two different types of name to correspond to integer and real values.

Fortran uses a rather strange convention here. Since the first character in a variable name must be a letter of the alphabet it determines whether it represents an integer or real value according to which particular letter is used. If the letter is one of I J K L M or N, then the variable name represents an integer value and is called an *integer* variable. If the letter is any *other* than one of these six, the name corresponds to a *real* variable. So

    I   J4   LENGTH   NUMBER   are *integer* variable names, and

    A   C6   HEIGHT   SIZE2   are *real* variable names.

The integer and real values which can be written into programs and stored in the computer are naturally exactly those values which can also be used as data for the program to take in or for results for the program to print out.

The practical preparation of a program for the computer

When the Fortran language was designed, there was only one way of using a computer. The program was written on a coding form and converted later into punched cards (or punched paper tape) to be put into the computer. The results were available only in print on a fixed style of output paper. It is often still convenient in the early stages of programming to do it this way and the details relevant to a particular computer installation are provided in appendix 1. Certainly this method of using the computer is implicit in many of the detailed considerations in programming.

Since those early times, there has been a great increase in the variety of computer input and output methods. It is becoming more and more common for programs to be called into execution by users at individual terminals attached to a central computer, and for the results to be relayed back to the terminal, to be typed out, or displayed on a visual display unit (VDU). Although this method of use increases the value of many programs, it has no effect on the way in which programming needs to be presented here.

Structure of a program statement in Fortran

Each of the operations specified in the program plan has to be *coded* into the Fortran language as a sequence of Fortran *statements*. The word 'statement' is used instead of 'instruction' because certain of the statements provide information to the computer rather than instructing it to do anything. The arrangement of a Fortran statement is determined by the way it will fit on a punched card and it is most easily described by looking at the card first.

There is room for 80 characters altogether on the card and this is split into four sections, each with a different purpose.

    Positions 1- 5   statement number
                                  position 1 can also be used for a comment indicator
    Position   6   continuation indicator
    Positions 7-72   statement body
    Positions 73-80   reference

The use of each section will become clearer as the different statements are described, but we can discuss some general points now.

The statement number is somewhere between 1 and 99999 and a statement number is used on the front of certain types of statement.

The comment indicator is 'C' in position 1. If a 'C' is punched there it means that the contents of the particular card are to be regarded as a programmer's comment and not to be taken as an instruction to be carried out. Comment cards are used to document a program so that it becomes more understandable to someone reading it. They give invaluable information and assistance when checking a program or looking for errors.

The continuation indicator position is used only when a statement gets too lengthy to get on to one card. If any character other than zero is put in that position it means that the contents of that particular card are to be regarded as a continuation of the *previous* card's content. So most cards have nothing in that position.

Positions 7 to 72 carry the main body of the Fortran statement, while positions 73 to 80 are not used as part of the Fortran program at all. If the programmer requires it, a reference name and number can be placed in those columns to indicate where the card belongs, a good practice which is particularly useful when a stack of cards is dropped on the floor.

Structure of a data card in Fortran

The previous section has described the way of laying out a Fortran statement against the background of punched card preparation. Data which is to be processed by a program is often prepared on punched cards as well. In this case however, it should be noted carefully that the way in which the data is laid out is not related in any way to the structure of a Fortran statement. The way in which the data is to be laid out on the card is determined by the form of the statements which are used to take it into the computer, and as long as these are mutually compatible, the data can be laid out in any way over the 80 positions that the programmer requires.

Writing conventions

To avoid ambiguity, it is recommended that the following convention is adopted in all handwritten Fortran statements:

    letter   O   I   Z
    numeric   Ø   1   2

and that extra care is taken to distinguish between the characters 7 and T, and 5 and S.

Examples

4.1 Classify the following constants as real, integer or invalid:

    1. 1.ØØ6   5. 1,2Ø5,672   9. Ø
    2. 2684   6. -15   10. Ø.Ø
    3. 152.0   7. 19.Ø   11. .7523
    4. +37.8532   8. -87.435.21   12. Ø.Ø34,529,6

4.2 Classify the following names as integer variable, real variable or as invalid:

    1. BOLTS   5. 14TH   9. SAVINGS
    2. RATE   6. JOB NO   10. PENCE
    3. NO   7. J3   11. A1B2C3
    4. TYPE 2   8. COST.   12. K

5 Reading and writing

Although it is possible to write programs which create interesting results without processing 'data' (such as printing out all the prime numbers up to a certain size), the majority of programs require to take in some sort of data to work with. The calculating power of the computer cannot start to be applied without it. Correspondingly there are some very useful programs which do no arithmetic at all, such as those which print out a series of name and address labels using information which may be held in the computer permanently. Certainly all programs must provide some sort of result. So we shall first look at how to get data in and out of the computer, before turning to calculation.

Reading information

For the sake of concreteness, let us assume that the input data is available in punched card form. A typical punched card may contain a single number, say 456.

Let us consider what the computer must be told to enable it to take in this number. First, it seems useful to use the word READ somewhere. Then, referring to the block diagram of the computer, it will be seen that there may be many input devices connected to a single computer. Remembering that the program is written as if it were already in the computer, with the data it is to work on still outside, it is clearly necessary to specify the particular input device from which the data is to come. This is done by using a different number for each of the possible input sources. In practice, most programs make use of a standard input number if the data is in punched card form, and by some historical process this has become 5.

When the input value has been read from the punched card then it must be provided with a storage space to hold it until it is required in the calculations. Finally, it is necessary to describe how the data value is laid out on the data card. It may be at the front, somewhere in the middle or even at the end of the card. To provide all this information, we require to write *two* Fortran statements in the program. Assume that the number 456 is laid out on the data card in the first three positions. To take in the number from the input card the statements required are

```
      READ(5,32)IVALUE
   32 FORMAT(I3)
```

There are two statements, a READ statement and a FORMAT statement. If the READ statement is provided on a punched card, the word READ can start in the seventh position along the card. After READ comes a pair of brackets enclosing two numbers. The first one, already discussed, tells the computer where the data value 456 is going to come from and we can use the number 5 for now. The second number in the brackets will be found to be repeated at the front of the FORMAT statement. It is a statement number, whose job is to tie the READ and FORMAT statements together. In the example they have been written down next to each other, but they may be separated by other statements and so the same 'flag', in this case the number 32, is attached to each. It could be any number between 1 and 99999.

Following the closing bracket in the READ statement is a variable name, and this is the part where we specify the place to store the number which is going to be read in. IVALUE is an integer variable name because it is an integer which is going to be read in.

Turning to the FORMAT statement, we have the statement number on the front within the first five positions of the punched card and the word FORMAT starts in the seventh position. Following that is something inside a pair of brackets. It is useful to see these brackets as enclosing a 'picture' of the layout of the input data on the input card. Notice that the actual data is not given in the FORMAT statement, for that is only available on the input card (it may change each time the program is used); it is the way in which it is arranged, provided in a suitable coded form. In this example the code is I3. The I code stands for integer and the three gives the number of characters making up the number 456, three digits. I is the first example of several special code letters used with special meaning in the FORMAT statement. Notice that when it is used there it has no connection with possible variable names I or I3, which may well be used in other parts of the program. However, it is still not clear how the FORMAT statement has specified that the number is to be found in the *first* three positions on the card. The convention is that the opening bracket in the FORMAT statement represents the front end of the card. Since the I3 is the *first* thing mentioned after the opening bracket it refers to the *first* three positions on the card.

The result of this pair of statements is therefore to place the value 456 into the storage space set apart for the integer variable IVALUE. The same pair of statements would work for *any* value in the first three positions of the data card. If we required to give IVALUE a greater value than 999 then we could write

    FORMAT(I6)

which would enable us to provide any value up to 999999 on the data card. Notice that the size we allow on the data card is not connected with the space taken up in storage. Every integer name is given the same amount of storage as explained previously, and spare space is filled up with zeros. What happens if we wish to put on the data card a smaller number than the FORMAT statement specifies? Then the convention is that blank spaces count as zeros. So the sequence blank, blank, 123, blank with a format code of I6 will be interpreted as 1230. A plus or minus sign can be placed in front of the number as long as space has been allowed in the format code and if there is no sign it is assumed positive.

Now let us consider taking in two integer values from the same data card. A new problem arises because it does not seem sensible to put the two numbers right next to each other. So it seems that we need something in the FORMAT statement to allow us to leave a space on the card. This is provided by the X format code. Possible statements to read in the two numbers are

    READ(5,32)IVALUE,KVALUE
 32 FORMAT(I3,2X,I3)

This enables us to put the first value in the first three positions of the card, to follow it up with *two* blanks, and then put the second value in the following three positions. Since we are taking in two values, we require two integer variables to give the values to, and these are provided in the READ statement, separated by a comma. The *first* name specified in the READ statement will receive the *first* value specified in the FORMAT statement, and so on. The X format code actually specifies that a position is to be ignored. If the data card has a particular character in that position, it will be neglected. The fact that we write 2X to indicate two positions to be ignored rather than X2 is just a peculiarity of Fortran. Notice that the FORMAT statement does not have to specify what is to be done with all 80 positions on a card. We can put in the closing bracket just as soon as everything of interest has been specified.

Real values can be specified in a similar way to integers. The relevant format code is F (originally standing for 'floating point', an engineer's way of describing the storage of a real number). For example, the number 45.678 can be read in from the first six positions in the card by

    READ(5,32)RVALUE
 32 FORMAT(F6.3)

The F code in the FORMAT statement explains that a real value is in that position. The 6 after it explains that there are six characters involved in the representation of the number on the card. Notice that the decimal point in the value must be counted as one of the characters. The new feature is the .3 following F6. The point confirms that a real number is being processed, the 3 says that there are *three* figures behind the decimal point in the number on the data card. It seems reasonable to suppose that this fact could have been detected by an inspection of the number coming off the data card, but this over-specification becomes sensible if it is pointed out that the information between the brackets in the FORMAT statement is treated as a little program to take the data from the input card, *before* the actual values on it are known. In the present example, the value 45.678 is given to the real variable called RVALUE.

In the same way as with integers we can read two (or more) values from the same data card. The statements

```
   READ(5,32)RVALUE,TVALUE
32 FORMAT(F6.3,3X,F5.1)
```

will read in a card such as:

with *three* spaces between the two values.

Naturally, we can combine real and integer values on the same data card, as long as we provide the types of variable name in the READ statement and the correct 'picture' in the FORMAT statement, for example:

```
   READ(5,67)RVALUE,IVALUE
67 FORMAT(F6.3,4X,I5)
```

A very reasonable question may arise here. How can we make available the right amounts of space on the data card if we don't know what values are to be presented later to the program as data? The answer is we can only make a reasonable estimate and since smaller numbers can always be coped with, it is best to err on the larger size. Why not then set aside the maximum possible space for each variable on the data card? If we try to do that, then there may not be enough space on the card to hold all the data we wish to put on it.

Writing information

In many ways the writing out of information is the *converse* of reading it in, and so the structure of the required statements is similar.

It seems good to use the word WRITE, and then the computer requires similar information as for reading. First, it requires to know on which of the possibly many output devices the message is to appear. Here it is conventional to use the number 6 to indicate the usual output printer. Then it requires to know where the value to be written out is to be obtained from. Finally, it requires information on how the result is to be spaced out on the printed page. Let us consider the output of a particular number, say 128, which is the value of the integer variable IVALUE. Suitable statements are

```
      WRITE(6,33)IVALUE
   33 FORMAT(1X,I3)
```

    The WRITE statement is just like the READ statement. The 6 tells the computer on which device to print the result, the 33 ties the WRITE statement and the corresponding FORMAT statement together, the variable name after the closing bracket says where the output value is coming from. The FORMAT statement is similar but with one extra feature. Inside the brackets is a 'picture' of the way information is to be laid out on the line of printed output. The I3 means that an integer value with three digits is to be placed in the first three positions of the output line. Then what about the 1X? By analogy with the meaning of 1X in the reading FORMAT statement, we would expect that it meant "leave a single space on the line before the three-digit integer". If it had occurred *after* the I3 it would mean just that, but in its position as the very *first* piece of information in the writing FORMAT statement it has a special meaning: "move the printer paper on from the line just printed to a new line and then print the *rest* of the information specified in this FORMAT statement on the new line". Exactly how this works will be explained later, but for now it is only necessary to remember to put 1X in the first position in *every* writing FORMAT statement. Apart from this position, the format codes which can be used have exactly the same meaning as with the READ statement.

    If we wish to print out two integers on the same line with two spaces between them, say the values of IVALUE and KVALUE, then suitable statements are

```
      WRITE(6,33)IVALUE,KVALUE
   33 FORMAT(1X,I3,2X,I3)
```

Notice that the second use of the X format code means, "leave two spaces on the line". Similarly two real values can be printed out with

```
      WRITE(6,33)RVALUE,TVALUE
   33 FORMAT(1X,F6.3,2X,F6.3)
```

and any combination of real values, integer values and spaces can be printed out as long as corresponding variable names are provided in the WRITE statement. Naturally, the values which are to be printed out must have been assigned to the corresponding variable names by some previous statements in the program.

    Now a question arises rather similar to that suggested in the case of the READ statement. How can we specify the correct number of characters for an output value in the FORMAT statement if we do not know how big the results is going to be? The answer is similar to that given previously. A reasonable estimate must be made, based on previous experience and possibly some rough hand calculations. Again, there is no problem if the answers are smaller than expected, since there will just be more space around them. If they are larger than can be printed out, then most computer operating systems print out a warning message and the FORMAT statement can be adjusted later. The format code for printing out a particular variable can be seen as representing a 'window' of a certain width through which we can 'see' a part of the contents of the storage assigned to the corresponding variable name. It is up to us to get the width of the window right.

Multiple READ and WRITE

A FORMAT statement can be associated with more than one READ statement *provided* the data lies in the same positions. For example, if we wish to read two successive data cards, such as:

and to store the information in ITEM1, COST1, ITEM2, COST2 we can do so with the following statements:

```
      READ(5,12)ITEM1,COST1
      READ(5,12)ITEM2,COST2
   12 FORMAT(I5,5X,F10.2)
```

Note that the FORMAT statement could equally as well have been placed in order between the two READ statements.

The same principle applies to WRITE statements and the printing out of results on successive lines using the same layout.

A complete program

Now that we have available the means to read data and to write it out, it is possible to construct a complete program. It is not suggested that a program which does no calculation at all is very useful, but it enables us to obtain experience in creating a complete program and using a computer system.

Let us consider a program which does nothing more than taking in a single integer number and writing it out again. Suitable statements are

```
      READ(5,22)IVALUE
   22 FORMAT(I3)
      WRITE(6,33)IVALUE
   33 FORMAT(1X,I3)
```

What extra is required to turn this into a program? As indicated previously, it will be necessary to provide information to the computer system about what is to be done with the program, and this will be discussed in the next section. However, there are further Fortran statements still to be added. First, every program has to be told when to stop and it seems natural to use the statement

```
      STOP
```

which will be placed in sequence after the WRITE statement. It seems that this statement will bring any program to a close and not much else can be done afterwards. But in Fortran we require yet another statement to mark the finish of a program, and that is

```
      END
```

It may appear that this is merely duplicating the request to stop, but in fact it is fulfilling an entirely different purpose. STOP is a command which is obeyed when the program is at work, having been previously translated into machine code and set into execution. END is a statement which does not get translated into machine code; it informs the translating operation that there are no more statements in this program and so the translation process can treat all the statements up to this point as a single program and get to work on the translation. Since every Fortran program must be translated, there must always be an END statement in the very last position in sequence. There should always be a STOP statement as well, but we shall see that it does not always require to come just before the END card. In fact, there may be several STOP statements in different places in the program, although only one of them will be obeyed in a particular execution of the program. We can now present the first complete program

```
      READ(5,22)IVALUE
   22 FORMAT(I3)
      WRITE(6,33)IVALUE
   33 FORMAT(1X,I3)
      STOP
      END
```

It may seem that a small program like this is rather obsessed with getting finished, and certainly one would expect something more in the way of an introduction. What about complementary statements to STOP and END?

The fact that a start statement is not required is due to the very general programming convention that, since the statements are always given to the computer in a fixed sequence, then the *first* statement that asks for something to be done will be the *first* to be carried out. After that, the statements are carried out in the order in which they have been written down *unless* some particular statement asks for this rule to be suspended.

Examples

5.1 A card contains the two numbers

    -20   346

starting in columns 1 and 7 respectively. Write down the necessary READ and FORMAT statements required to read the values into storage locations IVALUE and JVALUE.

5.2 Describe the layout of the data card that the following statements will read

```
      READ(5,10) AVALUE, BVALUE, CVALUE
   10 FORMAT(F6.3,3X,F10.4,2X,F7.3)
```

5.3 Pick out four errors in the following pair of statements

```
      READ(5,15) AX,NEXT.NUMBER,REX
   15 FORMAT(3X,I4,I6,7X,F7.2,F8.1
```

5.4 The following variables have been given these values

```
   DIST     10.12
   BRED      6.053
   ICOUNT   20
   FRACT     0.006
```

Give the necessary WRITE and FORMAT statements to output these values allowing a width of ten columns and with ten spaces between each field.

5.5 Describe the line of output produced by the statements

```
      WRITE (6, 1500) M, X, N, Y
 1500 FORMAT (6X, I2, 3X, F8.4, 2X, I6, 4X, F8.3)
```

where   -3845 is the value in M
           280 is the value in N
         22.3456 is the value in X
         128.2937 is the value in Y

Program Exercise 1

In a small survey of 3 children, the sex, height, weight and age of each child is noted. A data card is then produced for each child in the following form:

COLUMN 1	For a boy a 1 is punched. For a girl a 2 is punched.
COLUMN 2-5	These columns are left blank.
COLUMN 6-10	The weight of the child is recorded here as an integral number of pounds.
COLUMN 11-15	These columns are left blank.
COLUMN 16-20	Height is punched here as a real number of feet. It is assumed known correct to three decimal places.
COLUMN 21-25	These columns are left blank.
COLUMN 26-30	The age of the child is punched here as a real number of years (i.e. in the form 2.65). It is assumed that the age is less than 15 and that it is correct to two decimal places.

Write a program to input (read in) the three data cards, putting the sexes in ISA, ISB, ISC, the ages in AGEA, AGEB, AGEC, the heights in HIGHA, HIGHB, HIGHC, and the weights in IWAYA, IWAYB, IWAYC. Now output (write out) these values in the form:

```
ISA         ISB         ISC
AGEA        AGEB        AGEC
HIGHA       HIGHB       HIGHC
IWAYA       IWAYB       IWAYC
```

6 Arithmetic

Introduction

Probably most people use computers to compute with, that is, to carry out numerical calculations. In this chapter, we show how to specify in Fortran arithmetic operations which produce numerical results for later output.

A simple example

The most common statement for specifying arithmetic operations in Fortran is the *assignment* statement. A typical example of this statement is

    A=B+C

The statement refers to three variable names, A, B, and C, each of which identifies the storage location of the current value associated with that variable. The storage locations are conventionally of a fixed size in any particular machine but vary between machines. The operations which take place as a result of this statement are in the following sequence. The current values of B and C are taken from storage, they are added together in the arithmetic processor of the machine, and the result is put into the storage location associated with A.

Notice that we are really doing two different things. First, we are obtaining values associated with variable names and combining them arithmetically. Then, when a single result has been produced, we are *assigning* that value to another variable and storing it in the location corresponding to that variable name. This process of assignment is rather obscured by the use of the 'equals' sign because in Fortran the equals sign does *not* do the same job as the equals sign in ordinary mathematics. In algebraic calculations we may write

    B+C=A

and this will mean exactly the same as

    A=B+C

In Fortran, however, the purpose of the variable names is very different, according to their position to the left or right of the equals sign. The right hand side of an arithmetic statement leads to the production of a single numerical result. The *sole* purpose of the left hand side is to provide the name of a location in which this result is to be stored. The statement

    B+C=A

is accordingly meaningless in Fortran since there is no storage location associated with "B+C". If the words "is replaced by" are used instead of "equals" whenever the '=' sign is encountered there can never be confusion over its use.

It is important also to notice what happens to the values of the variables when an arithmetic statement is performed. During the calculation, the variables on the right hand side of the statement are referred to, that is, a *copy* of the current value of each variable is taken from the relevant storage location and used in the arithmetic operation. This process leaves the original value of the variable unchanged and it may be referred to again and again in further arithmetic statements. However, the single variable name on the left hand side of the equals sign provides a location to receive a new result and so its original value is necessarily destroyed. Notice also that it disappears *completely*. Every arithmetic operation always involves the complete contents of a particular storage location. If the location A contains 513976.85249 to start with and the new value we wish to put in is 1.3, then we can assume that 1.3 is represented as 000001.300000 with as many noughts as are required to fill a storage location completely. Therefore the original very large number is completely replaced by the much 'smaller' 1.3.

Each of the foregoing points is well illustrated by the very common Fortran statement

    N=N+1

This is not very meaningful in ordinary arithmetic; in Fortran, we are instructed to obtain the value of N, say 53; to add one to it, giving 54; and then to put that value back in N. In this case, the original value of N is destroyed, because N is specified on the left hand side of the equals sign.

Arithmetic expressions

A very simple example of the arithmetic statement has been described which involved only addition. The other arithmetic operations which can be specified on the right hand side of an arithmetic statement are those familiar in ordinary arithmetic.

+	addition	A+B means 'add A to B'
-	subtraction	A-B means 'subtract B from A'
*	multiplication	A*B means 'multiply A by B'
/	division	A/B means 'divide A by B'
**	exponentiation	A**B means 'raise A to the power B'

Notice that the limited set of different symbols available in Fortran has made necessary the use of an asterisk for multiplication and, since there are no superscript forms of letters or digits, a^b (a to the power b) has become A**B.

The arithmetic operators can be used freely in combination to build up as complicated an expression as required, such as:

    A+B-C*D+E/F

As soon as more than one arithmetic operation is specified however, the problem of the order in which the operators are carried out raises difficulties.

In agreement with everyday algebra, the expression

    A+B*C

should mean

    'Multiply B by C and add the result to A', *although* this is not the order in which the operators are written down.

It is also necessary to be able to specify sub-expressions by enclosing them in brackets. This implies that the expression inside the brackets is to be evaluated before attending to operations outside the brackets.

This can be arranged by defining a hierarchy of operations as shown below:

Level 1	sub-expression contained in brackets
Level 2	exponentiation (raising to a power)
Level 3	multiplication, division
Level 4	addition, subtraction

Then the general rule applies that all operations at the first level are performed before those at the second level and so on. If more than one operation at the same level is specified, then evaluation proceeds from left to right *across* the expression.

The hierarchy rule can be demonstrated by considering the evaluation of

    A+(B+C)/D-E*F+G**H

At level 1, the expression in brackets is dealt with. B is added to C and the result is stored temporarily. Since there are no other brackets in the expression, level 1 operations are complete and level 2 operations proceed from left to right. Accordingly G is raised to the power H and stored for later use. At level 3, the value of B+C, recovered from storage, is divided by D and again the result is stored temporarily. The next step, still at level 3, is to multiply E by F and place the result in another temporary location. This completes the level 3 operations. Next, at level 4, the operations of addition and subtraction are carried out, using values from temporary storage as required, until a single final result is obtained. The process is illustrated graphically as follows:

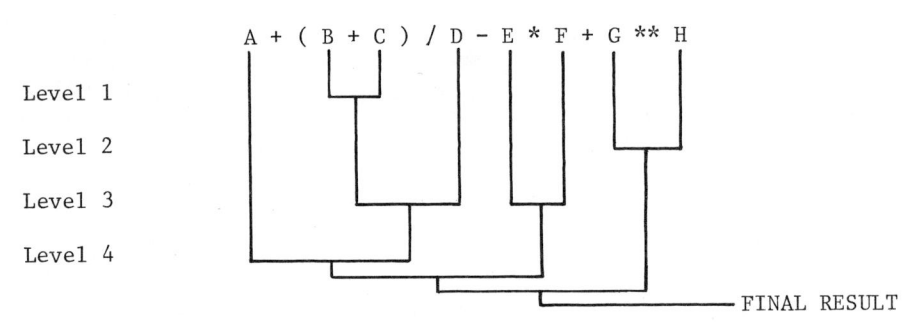

```
              A + ( B + C ) / D - E * F + G ** H
Level 1
Level 2
Level 3
Level 4
                                            FINAL RESULT
```

Although it can be seen that a complex sequence of operations takes place during the evaluation of a complicated arithmetic expression, they are carried out entirely automatically, and there is no need for the user to assign the temporary storage or control the sequence in any way. It is necessary only to be aware of the hierarchy of operations and to ensure that the arithmetic expression is written in the correct order and with a suitable use of brackets to ensure a correct evaluation.

In the example just described, variable names using one alphabetical character have been used for brevity. Each one of these could have been replaced by any legal Fortran real variable name or by a real constant. Thus the sequence of operations just described would have taken place in exactly the same way if the following expression had been provided:

ABLE+(B123+3.56)/1.793-2.1*CLOOT+DAVE**2.0

It will have been noticed that all examples of arithmetic expressions given so far have involved *real* variables and constants. In fact, all that has been said in this chapter so far is correct if an *integer* variable or *integer* constant is substituted for each occurrence of a real variable or constant, so that the expression is made up exclusively of integer variables and constants. We may write, for example:

J=K+L*M-N**2

However, a problem arises when we consider division with integers. It is clear that the normal process of division between integers will not produce an integer as a result, except in special cases where the denominator divides the numerator exactly. It is therefore necessary to define a special process of integer division in Fortran as follows: if, for example, I has the value 5 and J is 4, then I/J has the value 1. This is just as if, before the division, I and J had been converted to real numbers and the result, which was the real number 1.25 had been converted to an integer by simply cutting off the decimal point and all the figures after it. Likewise if I is 7 and J is 4, then the result is also 1.

An example of the way in which integer divisions can be used is illustrated by the following method of converting NMETRS, an integer number of metres, to kilometres and metres, assuming it is necessary to place the number of kilometres and metres in the separate storage locations KMETRS and METRES.

KMETRS = NMETRS / 1000
METRES = NMETRS - KMETRS * 1000

Mixed expressions

Since integer and real values are stored in different ways inside the computer, the mixing together of the two types in a single arithmetic expression is not permitted. For instance

B/Y+I+2

is *not* permitted because B and Y are real variables, whilst 1 and 2 are integers. The only exception to this rule occurs when a real variable is raised to an integer power, such as:

    A**2

and this can occur as part of an expression involving other real variables such as:

    A**2+B+C*D

In this instance we are not attempting to use mixed arithmetic since A raised to the power 2 really means A*A.

Mixed assignment

The rules given in the previous section apply to arithmetic expressions which form the right hand side of an arithmetic statement. But it is not necessary for the variable name on the *left hand* side of the '=' sign to be of the same type as the right hand side. Thus it is permitted to write

    I=A+B

What happens in this case is that the right-hand side is evaluated to produce a real result. The left-hand side specifies that the result is to be stored as an integer. Therefore the real value (A+B) is converted to integer form and the result is stored in I.

The conversion of a real number to integer form can be viewed as the removal of the decimal point and all figures to the right of it. Note especially that there is no question of 'rounding' the real number, it is a simple truncation that is performed. Thus the real number 2.769 converted to integer form produces 2 as the result.

Returning to the evaluation of

    I=A+B

if A is 1.369 and B is 1.4 then I receives the value 2 after the operation.

The conversion of integer numbers to real form is dealt with in similar fashion and can be viewed as the addition of a decimal point and zeros to the right of it to the maximum number that can be represented in the storage location assigned to that value.

Therefore in the evaluation of

    A=I+J

if I has the value 2 and J is 3 then the right-hand side has the value 5. This is converted to the real number 5.000... and the result is stored in A.

Storage space and the accuracy of computation

The assignment statement in Fortran provides a powerful and natural way of specifying complicated calculations. The program statements look very like those that we are used to writing down for use outside the machine. However, this apparent similarity can be very misleading when we consider the accuracy of the calculations. It cannot be stressed too strongly that when we are using computers we are in the world of *finite* arithmetic. Every number stored in the machine is represented to a limited accuracy, depending on the machine in use (details are provided in appendix 2).

This produces some disturbing variations in the results that we may expect from even very simple calculations. For example, we would expect the result of dividing one by three and multiplying by three again to be one. But the arithmetic expression

    (1.0/3.0)*3.0

is unlikely to give the result 1.0.

The result of the division of 1.0 by 3.0 will be stored with the maximum accuracy of the machine, say 0.3333333333, and when this is multiplied by 3.0 we will obtain 0.9999999999 which is *not* the same as 1.0.

For many purposes, the difference between the actual and the expected result will appear insignificant, but this is a dangerous assumption in at least two particular situations. The first occurs when, for example, the result of the previous paragraph is *compared* with some other pre-specified number in the machine such as the value 1.0. In that case, there will be an inequality when we expect an equality, which is a very significant difference. The second problem occurs when the result of an arithmetic operation is used again to produce another result, and so on. The tiny differences soon mount up and can easily lead to totally meaningless results.

Another strange effect arises from the way in which numbers are represented in the computer. Plus zero and minus zero are not necessarily regarded as the same thing, and this can clearly have a profound effect on tests for equality.

There are no simple rules for overcoming all the problems of finite accuracy, and it is mainly a question of considering a particular numerical computation with respect to the particular characteristics of the computer being used.

The finite representation of computer numbers has also much wider implications. In particular, the 'best' method of computation from a mathematical point of view does not necessarily produce the 'best' results on the computer.

Examples

6.1 Re-write, if necessary, the following as Fortran expressions:

1. $A-(B+C)$
2. $A(B+C)$
3. $\dfrac{ARC}{6.0+CAL}$
4. $\dfrac{A+XN}{B}$
5. Ax^2+Bx+C
6. A^x+2
7. $\dfrac{A+23.2}{135.6D}$
8. $\dfrac{A*10^{30}}{-B*C}$

6.2 Which of the following are valid Fortran arithmetic statements?

1. A=B+C/D+E
2. B=P+25
3. A=(B+C)/(D+E)
4. B=A+X**2
5. Z=A(B+C)+D
6. B=A+X**2K
7. B=I+1
8. B=A+X**2*Y
9. X+Y=Z
10. I=(A*B*C)**X+2

6.3 Give the single arithmetic statement required to place in IX the integral part of the real value currently in X. For instance, if X contains 17.327 it is required to put 17 in IX.

6.4 Give the single arithmetic statement required to convert the integer in IBOX to its real equivalent and store it in RBOX.

6.5 Compute and store in RESULT the fractional part of the quotient obtained by dividing INT1 by INT2. For example, if INT1 contains 13 and INT2 contains 4, RESULT should be given the value 0.25 (the fractional part of 3.25).

Program exercise 2

In the survey on 3 children extend the first program to calculate the average age, weight and height of the children to two decimal places, *using the same three data cards*.

Also calculate the weight of each child in stones and pounds (14 pounds = 1 stone).

Finally, give the WRITE and FORMAT statements to output all these values.

7 Program flow

In our program plans we have described all problem solutions in terms of three structures: a simple sequence; a decision process involving two simple sequences, YES and NO; and a repetition process involving the repetition of a simple sequence or a combination of simple sequence and decision process.

So far, the programs we have been able to write are limited to simple sequences of statements that can only be performed once. As we have seen in earlier chapters, it is only worth using a computer if we can specify the solution of a problem in terms of the *repetition* of (nearly) the same sequence of instructions many times; and whenever we require repetition it is necessary to specify some decision-making process which will eventually bring the repetitions to an end. In this chapter, we show how to specify decision processes in Fortran, and also how to arrange for repetition in various ways.

Decision taking

Let us look at the decision process in relation to the implicit rule that instructions are carried out in sequence. The general form of the process can be written as

```
┌ Decision (Is .....?)
│     ┌
│ YES │  ─────────
│     │  ─────────
│     │  ─────────
│     └
│
│     ┌
│ NO  │  ─────────
│     │  ─────────
│     │  ─────────
│     └
│
│ ┌ *     (instructions following the decision process)
│ │   ─────────
└ └   ─────────
```

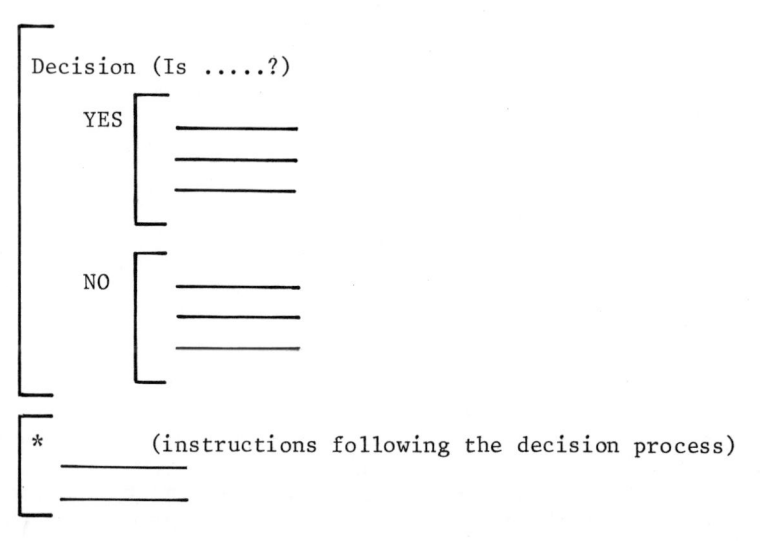

If the answer to the question is YES then the YES sequence is carried out and the instructions are obeyed consecutively. What happens after the last instruction in the YES sequence has been obeyed? If the computer is not told to do something else at that point, it will continue with the first instruction of the NO sequence, which is not very helpful. What we actually want to happen is that after completing the last YES instruction, the NO instructions will be ignored and the computer will continue with the first instruction *after* the complete decision process, marked with an asterisk (*).

The last instruction in the YES sequence therefore needs to be a new sort of instruction. Rather than asking for arithmetic to be done or values to be read in, it needs to instruct the computer where the *next* instruction is to be found, because it is *not* the next one written down. But before any suitable instruction can be given it is necessary to mark that 'next' instruction in some way so that it can be referred to. In the Fortran language this is done by putting a statement number in front of it, in the same way as we mark the FORMAT statement so that it may be referred to by a READ or WRITE statement. If the statement marked by an asterisk in the previous diagram is, for example:

```
    X=Y+Z
```

then we can mark it as follows:

```
    38 X=Y+Z
```

with statement number 38 for example. The Fortran statement to be written as the last of the YES sequence can now be specified. It is

```
    GO TO 38
```

So this part of the decision process is programmed as follows:

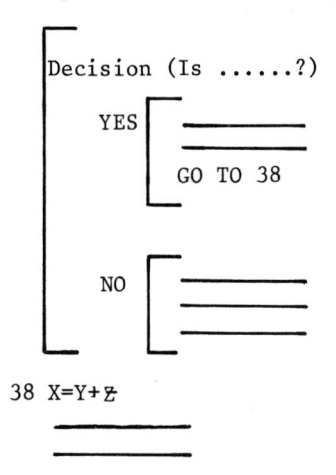

```
Decision (Is ......?)
    YES  ┌─────────
         │
         │ GO TO 38

    NO   ┌─────────
         │
         │
         │

38 X=Y+Z
─────────
```

What about the last instruction in the NO sequence? If we require at that point to go on to the statement marked 38 (which is normal) then it is not necessary to write anything, because we are immediately before statement 38 and so the implicit sequencing will take us automatically on to statement 38. We are now left with only the decision process itself to put into Fortran.

The statement to be used is called the *logical IF* and a particular example of this statement is as follows:

```
    IF(NEW.EQ.999) GO TO 46
```

We see that it consists of three parts: the word IF, which specifies the type of instruction as in the case of READ and WRITE; then, enclosed in the brackets, an expression which can be true or false; and, finally, an instruction to do something. How is this related to the question mark and the YES and NO sequences in the program plan?

The question is related to the expression in the brackets. We are saying in a rather special language "Is the value represented by the variable name NEW equal to 999?" What is specified after the closing bracket is clearly what is to be done if the answer is YES. So where do we write down what is to be done if the answer is NO?

The rather unbalanced arrangement in Fortran is that the NO instructions are written to *follow* the IF statement, that is on the next and successive lines.

If the answer to the question is YES then we are told to go to the statement with statement number 46 on the front. It is clear that this should be the first statement in the YES sequence. So far then, we have

```
       IF(NEW.EQ.999) GO TO 46
           ─────                ⎤
           ─────                ⎥  NO sequence
           ─────                ⎥
        GO TO 38                ⎦

    46     ─────                ⎤
           ─────                ⎥  YES sequence
           ─────                ⎥
           ─────                ⎦

    38 X=Y+Z                    ⎤
           ─────                ⎥  What happens after
           ─────                ⎥  the decision process
           ─────                ⎦
```

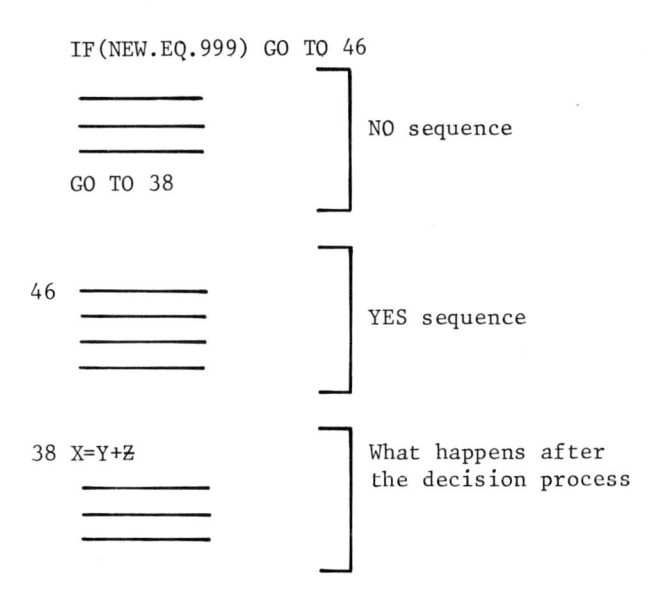

Having looked at a particular example of the logical IF statement, let us consider the general form. The word IF followed by brackets are the permanent features of the statement. Inside the brackets we are permitted to write any example of what is called a *logical expression*. The simplest form of expression is of the type already used in the example, two variables or constants separated by a *relational operator*. There are six of these, which describe very familiar numerical situations slightly disguised by a special shorthand form in Fortran, as shown below:

.EQ.	equal to
.NE.	not equal to
.LT.	less than
.LE.	less than or equal to
.GT.	greater than
.GE.	greater than or equal to

On each side of the relational operator we may have

a real variable

    A.EQ.B

or an integer variable

    I.EQ.J

or we may have one variable on one side and one constant of the *same* type on the other

    A.EQ.1.9
    I.EQ.3

We have to specify the same *type* of variable or constant on either side of the relational operator because the decision as to whether the relationship is true or false involves subtracting one value from the other and therefore has to obey the same rules as those for arithmetic expressions.

In connection with the warnings about finite accuracy in the last section of chapter 6, it should be pointed out that the use of .EQ. is best confined to integers which can be exactly equal. Real values can be dealt with in terms of 'greater than' or 'less than' which can be used to establish a small 'range of acceptance' around a particular value.

The CONTINUE statement

When we are using statement numbers in conjunction with GO TO statements it is good practice to have a special statement which clearly shows the start of a particular sequence of statements. Otherwise, it is easy to remove that statement when the program is altered and to forget to move the statement number to the new start of the sequence. For this purpose it is convenient to use the CONTINUE statement, which means "do not carry out any operation, but continue on to the next statement in the sequence". The front of each block of program will then look like

    38 CONTINUE

It may also be useful to follow the CONTINUE statement with a meaningful *comment* explaining the purpose of the block in order to give the program a degree of readability.

Decision taking and program loops

As well as providing a Fortran realization of the decision process the logical IF statement can be used to realize the third fundamental computing process, that is, repetition. Consider the following structure:

    38 CONTINUE
    ——————
    ——————

    GO TO 38

The statement number referred to in the GO TO statement does not occur after the GO TO but *before* it. Therefore when GO TO 38 is performed the program flow moves *back* to the CONTINUE statement, and unless the statements between CONTINUE and GO TO contain another GO TO statement then that sequence will be repeated endlessly. This process, called "getting into an infinite loop", is not very productive, but a slight amendment makes it fundamentally useful. If we replace GO TO 38 as follows:

    38 CONTINUE
    ——————
    ——————

    IF(I.LT.99)GO TO 38

and we arrange that the value of the integer variable I is modified every time we repeat the sequence, such as follows:

    I=0
    38 CONTINUE
    ——————

    I=I+1
    IF(I.LT.99)GO TO 38

Then it will be seen that the sequence is repeated a fixed number of times until I has reached the value 99 and then the program continues with the statement *after* the logical IF. By changing the numerical value in the logical expression I.LT.99 we can change the number of times that the sequence is repeated.

If the statements are arranged as in the previous example then note that the sequence between CONTINUE and IF will always be repeated whatever the value of the constant in the IF statement. If this is not satisfactory, then the logical IF must be moved to the beginning of the sequence to be repeated in some way such as the following:

    38 CONTINUE
       IF(I.GT.99)GO TO 44
    ——————

       GO TO 38
    44 CONTINUE

Notice that the relational operator is now 'greater than' and the loop is repeated if the logical expression is *false*. Notice also that there is nothing special about the numbers 38 and 44. Any two statement numbers would work in their place. However, the particular integer value 99 critically controls the number of times the loop is performed.

Now that we have available the means for making decisions and repeating sequences, we can create a great range of interesting programs. For example, the 'biggest number' solution worked out in Chapter 3 can now be programmed. The program plan was as follows:

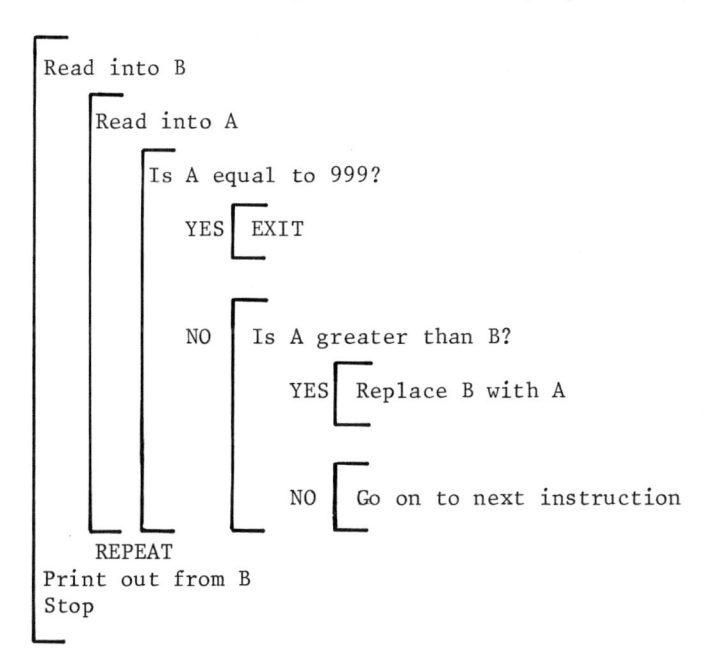

```
Read into B
    Read into A
        Is A equal to 999?
            YES  EXIT

            NO   Is A greater than B?
                    YES  Replace B with A

                    NO   Go on to next instruction
    REPEAT
Print out from B
Stop
```

We assume that the input data consists of integers less than 999 and the last card *is* 999. We will change the variable name A to NEW, which suggests that it *is* the new value being read in from each data card and we will change B to MAJOR which means greater and happens to be of integer type as well. The program can be written as follows:

```
       READ(5,22)MAJOR
33        CONTINUE
          READ(5,22)NEW
              IF(NEW.EQ.999)GO TO 44
                 IF(NEW.GT.MAJOR)GO TO 55
                    GO TO 66
55                  CONTINUE
                    MAJOR=NEW
66                  CONTINUE
          GO TO 33
44 CONTINUE
   WRITE(6,77)MAJOR
   STOP
22 FORMAT(I3)
77 FORMAT(1X,I3)
   END
```

Notice we have tried to follow the layout of the program plan which obviously helps in checking that the complete plan has been implemented by the program. The statement numbers have to line up of course, but the statements themselves can start anywhere on the line.

It will be clear that using the Fortran language does not permit us to follow the program plan exactly. For example, the NO and YES parts of the logical IF are interchanged with what is natural to write in the program plan. This *can* be overcome by changing the question which is asked to its opposite, for example from "Is N equal to 99?" to "Is N *not* equal to 99?". But this usually makes the final program more difficult to understand than through its disagreement with the program plan and is not recommended.

Now let us return to the third part of the logical IF statement. In the first example we used in this position

   GO TO 46

which is an ordinary Fortran statement capable of standing on its own. This is true more

33

generally as well. After the brackets in the logical IF we may write *any* single executable statement apart from another logical IF. For example:

    IF(A.LT.0.0)A=-A

Here we have written a rather unusual arithmetic assignment statement after the brackets.

In fact it is not usually convenient to put any statement other than a GO TO in this position since the usual decision process involves a YES sequence and a NO sequence of several statements each. Only *one* of these sequences is performed and then we rejoin the simple sequence following the decision process. But if the statement following the bracket of the logical IF is not a GO TO then after it has been performed we have no choice but to go on to the next statement which is the one immediately following the logical IF. This is equivalent to saying that the YES sequence consists of only one statement (the one which follows the bracket of the logical IF) and the NO sequence is empty, that is, there is nothing special to be done if the answer is NO and we rejoin the main sequence immediately following the logical IF statement. In practice, this is not so unusual and the 'biggest number' problem provides an example.

```
┌
│ IS NEW greater than MAJOR?
│       ┌
│   YES │ Replace MAJOR with NEW
│       └
│
│       ┌
│   NO  │ Do nothing.
│       └
└
```

becomes

        IF(NEW.GT.MAJOR)MAJOR=NEW
     66 CONTINUE
        ─────────

and we have got rid of two GO TO statements and a CONTINUE which seems a simplification.

Examples

    7.1 Construct the Fortran logical expression for each of the following:

        1.   P exceeds X   4.   C is equal to or less than D
        2.   Y exceeds 2.5   5.   K is equal to or exceeds L2
        3.   I is equal to J 6.   J is not equal to 99

    7.2 Write down in words the meaning of each of the following Fortran logical expressions:

        1.   X.LT.Y   4.   ED.GT.10.0
        2.   AB.NE.C   5.   MAX.LE.196
        3.   X.GE.B   6.   M1.EQ.999

    7.3 The variable x can have one of the three values 1, 2 or 3. When x=3, the variable y is zero; when x=1 or x=2, then y=3. Write a program sequence which calculates y for any value of x. Assume that x is given a value through a READ statement.

    7.4 The variable x is derived from y as follows:

        x = y if y is less than 1
        x = 0 if y equals 1
        x = y^2 if y is greater than 1

        Write a program sequence which calculates x for any value of y. Assume that y is given a value through a READ statement.

    7.5 Data consists of an unknown number of cards with an integer punched in column 1, and the rest of the card blank, except for the last card which has a 9 punched in column 10. Write a program to count the number of cards which have a 1 punched in column one of the card, and write out this value.

Program exercise 3

In the children's survey, it is required to find the following:

1. the number of boys in the survey
2. the number of girls in the survey
3. the average height, weight and age
4. the number of children above the age of five
5. the weight of each child in stones and pounds (14 pounds = 1 stone).

Write a program to provide this information. The data used has the same layout as previously but there are now more than three children in the survey. The final data card has nothing punched on it except a 9 in position 40.

You are advised to draw a program plan to help with the solution of the problem.

8 Repetition with subscripted variables

As we discussed in Chapter 2, 'repetition' in computing involves doing *nearly* the same thing many times, and often this involves repeating the *same* thing on *different* data. The 'finding the biggest' example in the previous section continually repeated the *same* READ statement which resulted in a succession of *different* data values being operated on. If we consider an apparently straightforward modification of this problem which prints out all of the input values that are above the *average* of all the readings then we encounter a new problem: it is necessary to read *all* the values into storage before we can calculate the average and then it is necessary to process *each* of the values again to compare it with the average and so decide whether or not to print it. A suitable section of program plan is

    Set TOTAL to zero

    ⎡ Read into NEW
    ⎣ Add NEW into TOTAL

    Repeat until all the values have been read in
    Divide TOTAL by the number of values to obtain AVERAGE

    ⎡ Obtain a data value and put into DATA
    ⎢ If DATA is greater than AVERAGE
    ⎢ then print out from DATA
    ⎣ otherwise do nothing

    Repeat for all data values previously read in
    Stop

For various reasons it is impractical to read the same collection of data values twice during the execution of a program and so we must store all the values in separate places as we read them in so that they can be used again. Now a new problem appears: while a continued repetition of the *same* READ statement provides a sequence of *new* pieces of data, if each of the incoming pieces of data is to be stored in a *different* location how can the *same* program statement used repetitively put the different pieces of data away in storage? Later on, we shall require a *single* statement, used repetitively, to be able to process each of the values again in sequence. The solution to both these requirements is provided by the idea of an array variable. It is possible to store a collection of values under a single name and this leaves only the problem of referring to each value individually when it is required. This is solved by the use of an *index* which is an integer number specifying which particular one of the collection is being referred to. The index is enclosed in brackets immediately following the variable name. For example, if the variable name A refers to a collection of (real) values, then A(2) refers to the second member of the collection, and A(18) refers to the eighteenth. Notice that A(2) is entirely different from the variable name A2 which refers to a single value. A2 and A18 have no connection with each other at all while A(2) and A(18) are intimately connected. However, this still does not appear to solve the problem of how the *same* instruction can refer sometimes to A(2) and sometimes to A(18). The answer is provided by replacing a specific number in the brackets by an integer *variable*. We can write A(K), which then refers to the Kth member of the collection A, according to the particular value that K has *when* the statement containing A(K) is executed. For example, if K has the value 8 at that time, then the eighth member of A is referred to. It is really the use of this concept together with the idea of repetition that makes programming worthwhile. Here is a possible sequence of instructions to put a succession of twenty values read from the input into storage:

```
      K=1
   25 CONTINUE
      IF(K.GT.2Ø)GO TO 76
      READ(5,32)A(K)
      K=K+1
      GO TO 25
   76 CONTINUE
```

```
   32 FORMAT(F6.3)
```

The value of the index K (any integer variable name will do) is set to one to start with and the first time that the READ statement is performed, it results in the first input value being stored in A(1). K is then set to two and when the READ statement is performed again, it results in the next input value being stored in A(2). The process continues with successive input values being stored in A(3), A(4) ... up to A(2Ø), when the loop terminates.

Here then, is how the *same* statement can refer to *different* pieces of data as it is repeated again and again. Notice again the difference between A(1), A(2), ... and A1, A2, ... Without the brackets it would be necessary to write down a different instruction every time we wished to read a new piece of data into storage, for example:

```
      READ(5,32)A1
      READ(5,32)A2
```

    etc.

This becomes totally impractical if we are processing thousands of items of data. There would be more effort involved in writing down the instructions than performing the original calculations without the aid of the computer.

However there is an extra problem still to overcome before the array variable A(K) can be used, and this concerns how a collection of data is stored. In all previous programs, it has not been necessary to say anything about the storage of variable values: if a variable name, say A3 is mentioned in the program, then a single position in storage is automatically made available for it during the translation of the program into machine code. However, if we write A(K) in the program, it is clear that the translating program cannot determine how many different values of K (and therefore different storage locations) may be involved. It is necessary to provide with the program information on how many places should be set aside to take the members of the collection A(or whatever array variable name we choose).

This is done by means of the DIMENSION statement. As an example, if we write

```
      DIMENSION A(23)
```

in the program, then twenty-three storage locations are set aside for the members of A. In this particular statement the numerical value in the brackets specifies the *largest* value expected. All members of the collection from A(1), A(2) ... up to the value specified in DIMENSION are then available for use. The figure in brackets is clearly an integer (there is no 2.5th member of an array) and Fortran requires it to be positive and non-zero. This implies that when a variable is used inside the brackets in the program, it will produce values which fit in with these rules. In fact, the failure to control this value provides one of the principal reasons for programs to go wrong. Notice that we cannot just avoid the problem by putting a very large integer in the DIMENSION statement. This would require the computer to set aside more storage space than was available for variables. Usually it is a question of making a reasonable estimate of the maximum number of data items which a given program will be required to work on. A large program may have values in the thousands.

The names of array variables follow the conventions for naming single variables in Fortran. The name can be of integer or real type (as distinct from the index inside the brackets) and this implies that all the members of the array will be integer, or all will be real.

We can now return to the original example which prints out all values of a collection which are above the average.

The data values are first placed in storage as in the previous example. At the same time, the values are added together to provide a cumulative total. This is divided by the number of values read in (assumed known) to produce the average value. A final repetitive sequence compares each member of the array in turn with the average value and prints out those which are greater. A possible sequence (not in any sense a 'good' program) to realize this is given now.

```
      DIMENSION A(20)
      TOTAL=0.0
      K=1
   25 CONTINUE
      IF(K.GT.20)GO TO 35
      READ(5,33)A(K)
      TOTAL=TOTAL+A(K)
      K=K+1
      GO TO 25
   35 CONTINUE
C
      CENTRE=TOTAL/20.0
C
      N=1
   45 CONTINUE
      IF(N.GT.20)GO TO 55
      IF(A(N).LE.CENTRE)GO TO 65
      WRITE(6,44)A(N)
   65 CONTINUE
      N=N+1
      GO TO 45
   55 CONTINUE
      STOP
   33 FORMAT(F3.1)
   44 FORMAT(1X.F3.1)
      END
```

The impression this program gives is of a most unpleasant complexity, which would be heightened if we added the necessary statements to make the output intelligible. Later on, we shall see how to achieve these results with many fewer statements and how to improve the legibility of longer programs.

Two-dimensional arrays

Sometimes it is useful to view a collection of values as a two-dimensional arrangement such as the following:

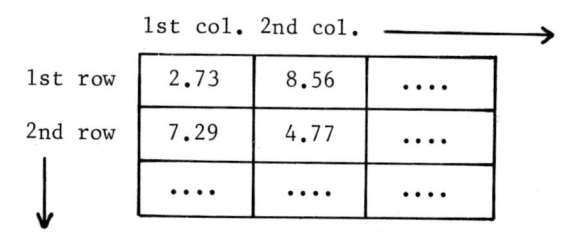

	1st col.	2nd col.	→
1st row	2.73	8.56	....
2nd row	7.29	4.77	....
↓	....	....	....

In Fortran we can provide *two* indices to indicate the position of an individual member in an array of this type as follows:

	1st col.	2nd col.	→
1st row	A(1,1)	A(1,2)	....
2nd row	A(2,1)	A(2,2)	....
↓	....	....	....

The first index refers to which row the number is in, the second to which column.
We can specify the necessary storage space by a statement like

    DIMENSION A(30,20)

which asks for 600 storage locations (30 x 20) to be set aside and the array A will then have thirty rows and twenty columns. Computations will then be able to specify, for example:

A(J,K)

which will process the member of A in the Jth row and the Kth column according to the particular values of J and K at the time. This type of array can naturally be given an integer variable name as well, when all members of the array will be integers. Examples of the use of such arrays will be given later.

The following points need to be remembered when using arrays:

1. The variable name of the array has the same specification as an ordinary variable name.
2. If the variable name is an integer type, all the numbers stored in the array must be integers; conversely, if the name is real, the numbers must be real.
3. The value of the index must be an integer and cannot be zero or negative.
4. Storage space is set aside for an array by use of a DIMENSION statement.
5. The DIMENSION statement has to be placed in the program before the first executable statement.
6. More than one array can be dimensioned in the same statement using commas to separate the array names.

Examples

8.1 Which of the following are valid subscripted variables?

1. A(-3)   4. JOB NO(10)   7. TAX(ID)
2. MANNO(5.0)   5. CAB(5.0)   8. INC(3,K)
3. DOE(J,K)   6. AREA(MINIMUM)   9. QUANT(H,K)

8.2 Store the 10th member of the array ALIST in the location called STORE.

8.3 Interchange the values in A(3) and A(4) without losing either value.

8.4 Write a program statement which multiplies the I-th member of the array A by the I-th member of the array B and stores the result as the I-th member of C.

8.5 Write a section of program which adds up all the elements of a two-dimensional array AR with 20 rows and 100 columns.

8.6 The array SUB has five members and the following interchange of values is to take place:

1. SUB (5) into SUB (1) and SUB (2)
2. SUB (4) into SUB (3) and SUB (5)
3. SUB (3) into SUB (4)

Write down the arithmetic statements necessary to complete the change.

Program exercise 4

In the survey it is required to find:

1. the number of boys in the survey
2. the number of girls in the survey
3. the average height, weight and age
4. the number of boys above the average height
5. the number of girls above the average height
6. the maximum height of the boys in the survey
7. the number of children above the age of five
8. the weight of each child in stones and pounds

Develop a program plan for this problem. Assume you are using the same data as in program exercise 3. (At a later stage you will be asked to write a complete program solution).

9 The control of repetition

The concept of repetition is so fundamental to computing that it seems sensible to have a separate statement to control it, rather than a combination of features that are provided primarily for decision making. In practice, the use of the GO TO statement to return control to a *previous* statement has been found to provide a principal source of errors in programming, and is best avoided as far as possible. The commonest method in Fortran is to make use of the DO statement and repetitions controlled in this way are nearly always referred to as 'DO loops'.

As an example, consider the reading of twenty data values into an array. A 'DO loop' can be specified as follows:

```
      DO 25 K=1,20
      READ(5,33)A(K)
   25 CONTINUE
```

By comparison with the use of the logical IF and GO TO statements to do the same thing, we see that the DO statement *includes* the complete mechanism for counting the number of repetitions. The statement itself has three parts: first, the operation name DO; then a statement number which tells us where the *other* end of the loop is (the front end is marked by the DO statement itself); and then an integer variable name, which serves as the 'loop counter'. In the example, K=1,20 means that K starts with the value one and each time the loop is repeated (in this case only a single READ instruction) K has one added to itself *until* the value following the comma is reached, in this case, 20. Clearly the K=1,20 part can only involve integers and the Fortran rule is that the loop counter can only take positive (and non-zero) values and that we can only count upwards.

Looking at the statement *inside* the DO loop, we see that the loop counter K has been used to specify which position of the array A we are reading into on a particular repetition of the READ statement. The loop counter can be used for this sort of job wherever we like *inside* the loop. For instance, the data values can be read in and also added together cumulatively by the following sequence:

```
      TOTAL=0.0
      DO 25 K=1,20
      READ(5,33)A(K)
      TOTAL=TOTAL+A(K)
   25 CONTINUE
```

The loop counter therefore can act as an ordinary integer variable, as long as we *only refer* to it to obtain its current value. It is clearly not sensible to interfere with its value by statements such as:

```
      K=K+1
```

since this will upset the automatic loop counting and testing procedure applied to it in the operation of the DO statement.

Notice that the CONTINUE statement with its attached statement number is used to mark the end of the loop. It is not *essential* to use the CONTINUE statement. In the example, the statement number 25 could have been attached to the last executable statement in the loop

```
   25 TOTAL=TOTAL+A(K)
```

However, this makes the program more difficult to read and is not recommended.

In the overall program sequence, the DO loop with its subsequence of statements, starting with the DO and finishing on the final CONTINUE counts as a single statement. When the DO loop has completed all its repetitions control is transferred to the statement *after* the last one inside the loop.

In the previous examples, the DO statement has been used to repeat a sequence a *fixed* number of times. It is possible for 'how many times' to be decided *inside* the program in two ways.

First, the top and/or bottom values of the 'loop counter' can be specified as integer variables, which are provided with values *before* the DO statement is executed. For example:

```
    DO 25 K=1,N
```

or

```
    DO 35 J=M,N
```

However, this does not enable us to decide when to terminate the loop *while* it is being performed. This is a common requirement, as for instance in reading in a collection of values with the end of them indicated by a special value, as in the 'biggest number' example. In this second method we have to employ a logical IF statement *inside* the loop. For instance, the 'biggest number' input sequence can be controlled as follows:

```
    DO 25 K=1,499
    READ(5,33)INEXT
    IF(INEXT.EQ.999)GO TO 35
    _____
    _____
 25 CONTINUE
    _____
    _____
 35 CONTINUE
    _____
    _____
```

The READ statement and the sequence following inside the loop as far as 25 CONTINUE are repeated until either there have been 499 repetitions *or* the condition in the logical IF statement is true, that is, the final record of the data file, containing 999, is encountered. In this case GO TO 35 is obeyed and control is transferred *out* of the loop to the statement

```
 35 CONTINUE
```

After that, the normal sequencing rules apply and the statement after 35 CONTINUE will be performed.

In this case it seems that there is not much advantage in using a DO statement rather than employing the method described before:

```
 25 CONTINUE
    READ(5,33)INEXT
    IF(INEXT.EQ.999)GO TO 35
    _____
    _____
    GO TO 25
```

especially if we do not need to make use of the value of the loop counter in the other statements inside the loop. However, the DO loop method is much to be preferred for the following reason: the DO statement forces us to provide a top limit to the number of repetitions and so if the logical IF fails to operate properly, say the '999' record is missing, then the program cannot go into an 'infinite loop'. If the 499 repetitions, for instance, have taken place and the '999' record has not been encountered, then the statements after 25 CONTINUE and before 35 CONTINUE can provide a warning message on the output pointing this out, and possibly arrange to stop the computation.

If the GO TO method of repetition is used, there is extra complication in arranging the record count and no obvious place for the error message. It also lays us open to all the potential dangers of allowing a GO TO to refer to a *previous* statement, which have been discussed before.

The 'biggest number' example shows that it is permitted to use a GO TO to jump out of a loop before it is completed by the normal operation of the DO mechanism. However, it is not permitted to use a GO TO outside the loop to jump inside. This is because if we do not enter the loop by obeying the DO statement, then the 'loop counter' is not set to its correct starting value and so the number of repetitions cannot be controlled properly.

In the DO statement already described the loop counter is incremented by one each time the loop is performed. If we require it to be incremented by some other (integer) value then this value can be written at the end of the DO statement. For example:

    DO 25 J=1,2∅,2

Since a principal advantage of using the DO loop is that it clarifies how many times the loop is to be performed it seems pointless to remove this advantage when an additional simple arithmetic statement will provide a suitable sequence of values to be used somewhere inside the loop for a particular purpose. In the previous example we can add an arithmetic statement to provide K with the required values thus preserving J as a loop counter.

    DO 25 J=1,1∅
    K=J*2-1
    ‾‾‾‾‾‾
    ‾‾‾‾‾‾
 25 CONTINUE

Nesting of DO loops

The sequence inside a DO loop may consist of any number of statements of any type. It may therefore include another DO loop.
This is particularly useful where data to be processed is arranged as a two-dimensional array. The following example is typical of many computations:

    DIMENSION A(7,9)
    TOTAL=∅.∅
    DO 25 J=1,7
       DO 35 K=1,9
       TOTAL=TOTAL+A(J,K)
 35 CONTINUE
 25 CONTINUE

Here, all 63 members of the two-dimensional array A are added together in TOTAL. The outer DO loop is encountered first. It starts on its first repetition with the value of J set to one. Then the inner DO LOOP comes into operation and with J equal to one there are nine repetitions of the inner loop with K taking the values 1, 2, 3, ...7, 8, 9. After this, the next statement 25 CONTINUE is executed and this happens to be part of the outer loop. The outer loop is then repeated with J taking the value 2, thus processing A(2,1), A(2,2),A(2,3),....A(2,9). The outer loop repeats in this way with all values of J up to 7 and so all values of array A are covered, row by row. There can of course be other statements inside the outer loop and the inner. Those in the outer loop only will be performed seven times in this example, those in the inner loop will be performed 63 times.
If we wish the 63 members of the two-dimensional array A to be referred column by column, we arrange the statements as follows:

    DIMENSION A(7,9)
    TOTAL=∅.∅
    DO 35 K=1,9
       DO 25 J=1,7
       TOTAL=TOTAL+A(J,K)
 25 CONTINUE
 35 CONTINUE

Remembering that a complete loop counts as a single statement in the sequence outside the loop, it is clear that ends of DO loops cannot overlap. One DO loop must be completely inside or completely outside another. It is possible for two DO loops to end on the same statement, but this is not good practice since it does not help the readability of the program.
In spite of these added complexities, the DO statement is an essential part of Fortran since it requests the maximum of computation with the minimum of effort in specification.

Here are some points to remember when using DO loops:

1. The loop counter can only take the form of an integer variable.
2. The initial and maximum values are each either a positive integer or a non-subscripted integer variable containing a positive integer value.
3. The loop counter and the controlling values may not be altered within the loop by the action of an arithmetic statement.

4. DO loops may be nested within each other but they may not overlap.
5. A transfer of sequence may not be made into a DO loop from outside, but a transfer may be made out before the loop counter has attained the maximum value.
6. Be careful not to use the same variable name as counters for two loops when one is nested in the other.

Examples

9.1 Given a set of not more than 100 data cards each with an integer number in the first 3 columns, ending with a 999 on the last card, write a program to print out the biggest number (i.e. *not* including the 999 end-of-data test card).

9.2 How would you amend the program for 9.1 above to handle up to 200 data records?

9.3 Write a program to calculate and print out in sequence the values of the powers of 2 from 10 to 20 (i.e. 2^n for n=10, 11, 12, ... 20).

Program exercise 4 (continued)

Using the program plan you have already developed, write a complete program solution to the problem specified on page 39.

10 Structuring the program - subprograms and parameters

The statements provided so far enable us to carry out all kinds of calculations which are or may be as complicated as we like. But the more complex the calculations, the more involved is the sequence of instructions, and if we allow the sequence to grow arbitrarily, we find that it becomes more and more difficult to construct it correctly in the first place and later amendments may become practically impossible. It is here that the principle of 'divide and conquer' comes to our aid.

If we are approaching the solution of a problem in the way suggested in Chapters 2 and 3, then we will have already split up a large problem into a series of more manageable sub-problems. It is now possible to write a series of *subprograms* to provide a solution to each of the subproblems in turn and then these subprograms must be related to each other in order to produce a solution to the complete problem. In Chapter 12 we will discuss this method in greater detail and relate it to the writing of *good* programs. In this chapter we will introduce the method of constructing subprograms and show how they can be related to each other.

Subprograms

The programs constructed so far have not had any clearly defined beginning. Conventionally, the program starts with a series of declarations such as DIMENSION and then we have a series of executable statements finished off by the END statement. Although a program arranged like this doesn't seem to need anything else, it is clear that when the program is split into subprograms, there will be a need to mark where each of the subprograms begins and ends. The principal way of doing this in Fortran is by use of the SUBROUTINE statement: a subprogram is enclosed between a SUBROUTINE statement and an END statement. Every subprogram needs a separate name so that it can be referred to and in Fortran these names follow the word SUBROUTINE and obey the same rules as variable names, except that the difference between real and integer is not relevant. A collection of subprograms will then have the following overall structure:

```
SUBROUTINE A
_____
_____

END
SUBROUTINE B
_____
_____

END
SUBROUTINE C
_____
_____

etc.
```

Let us consider how a program that is split up like this can be executed. One possible way is by executing the first subroutine written down, and then the second, and so on in order. In fact, as soon as we have available the concept of a separate subprogram, it proves most convenient to arrange the subprograms in a *hierarchy*. We have a chief program, which we call the *main* program and by executing this program we call into operation the subprograms in any order that we require. So the order in which the subprograms are written down is not important. The main program is clearly in a special position and it is necessary to have available in it a type of statement which can call a subprogram into operation. This is realized by the CALL statement:

```
CALL A
```

which brings into operation the subroutine with the name A. Now another problem arises.

The main program has called subroutine A into operation, but what happens when subroutine A has finished. By calling subroutine A the main program has handed over control to the subroutine, and when the subroutine's task is complete, the main program must gain control again. We clearly need something in the subroutine which, instead of stopping things entirely, returns control back to the main program. This is done by means of the following statement:

    RETURN

So a typical subroutine will look like

    SUBROUTINE A
    _____
    _____
    _____
    _____

    RETURN
    END

The RETURN statement clearly performs a function similar to STOP in the main program. But it is also possible to have a STOP in the subroutine. In this case when the STOP statement is performed in the subroutine the *whole* program will come to an end. However, this is not usually considered good programming practice. The main program should have final control, and that includes the decision when to stop. Notice that a subroutine requires an END statement since it is compiled separately from the main program and any other subroutine.

The next point concerns what happens after the RETURN statement is obeyed. Since a CALL statement at a particular point in the main program has brought the subroutine into operation, it seems natural that control should return to the statement *after* that CALL statement. So a main program with the form

    _____
    _____
    CALL A
    CALL B
    CALL C
    STOP
    END

will call subroutines A, B and C into operation in turn before stopping. Notice that the order in which the subroutines are called depends only on the sequence of statements in the main program. It has nothing to do with the order in which the subroutines are written down.

If the program is on punched cards, it is conventional to put the main program first. The subroutines can then be placed in any order. It is possible to call the *same* subroutines into operation many times from *different* places in the main program. This opens up a wider concept of the subroutine as a rather *generalized* sequence of statements, useful in many places, which is made to do a *particular* thing at any one place in a program. The mechanism for making its action specific is mainly concerned with data values and is dealt with in the next section.

Communication between subprograms I
_____

Splitting up a large program into a series of subprograms that are performed under the control of a main program is clearly useful to simplify a very complex job. But a problem arises when we consider how to handle the data which is to be processed. How can a series of nicely separated subprograms get at the *same* pieces of data without getting themselves all very mixed up again? Fortran provides two methods of doing this and as in the case of *real* and *integer* variables, it is not possible to avoid using both of them at some time or another. In this chapter we shall only consider the method which involves the use of *parameters*.

The CALL statement in the main program mentions explicitly which variable names are going to be involved when the subroutine is called into action. As an example consider the following sequence, which writes out a single value:

```
      WRITE(6,33)B
   33 FORMAT(1X,F6.3)
```

Let us turn this into a subroutine to print out a value but assume that the particular value is going to be determined in the main program. The subroutine can be written like this:

```
      SUBROUTINE PRINT(B)
      WRITE(6,33)B
   33 FORMAT(1X,F6.3)
      RETURN
      END
```

and the main program can have a statement

```
      CALL PRINT(X)
```

The new introduction in each case is a variable name in brackets following the subroutine name. Now this has nothing to do with an array index since PRINT is the name of a subroutine, not the name of a collection of variable values, and in this case it is a real value anyway. When used in the SUBROUTINE statement in this way, the computer is informed that the variable *value* indicated between the brackets is going to be shared by the subroutine *and* the main program. In this particular case, the value of B is going to be printed out, that value having been *provided* by the main program. Then why has the CALL statement not got the variable name B inside the brackets? The answer actually lies in the subroutine. We can see that the subroutine could just as well have been written as:

```
      SUBROUTINE PRINT(A)
      WRITE(6,33)A
   33 FORMAT(1X,F6.3)
      RETURN
      END
```

since exactly the same *operation* would be done. B or A or whatever we care to call it is known as a *dummy* variable. The actual name A or B is not important but its *position* is. We make use of the positional idea in the CALL statement as well, by allowing *any* variable name from the *main* program to be used in this position, for example Y, and the effect of that CALL statement is to make available the *value* of X from the main program wherever B is mentioned in the subroutine. For instance, if the current value of X in the main program is 6.334 then

```
      CALL PRINT(X)
```

will result in the value 6.334 being printed out by SUBROUTINE PRINT.

Another way of saying this is that during the operation of the subroutine the variable used in the CALL statement and the variable used in the SUBROUTINE statement are *identified*. In fact, when the subroutine is called into operation it is given the *address* of X, to be used wherever B is mentioned in the subroutine. We normally try to avoid describing detailed operations inside the computer but, in this particular case, the realization that the *same* storage location is being called X in the main program (or whatever name is used in the CALL statement) and B in the subroutine provides an essential insight.

Consider another example:

```
      SUBROUTINE INPUT(A)
      READ(5,22)A
   22 FORMAT(F6.2)
      RETURN
      END
```

with its associated CALL statement

```
      CALL INPUT(X)
```

Here the value of A is *obtained* by the READ statement and is being *handed over* to the main program for use in later calculations. Remembering that during the operation of the subroutine, the location of X is handed over to the subroutine to be used wherever A is mentioned, it is clear that on return to the main program X will have been given the value which has been read in during the operation of the subroutine.

Although the same variable name happens to have been used in CALL PRINT(X) and CALL INPUT(X), it is clear that the main program will use X in very different ways in each case. The use of

    CALL PRINT(X)

presupposes that a value for X has already been computed in the main program, while

    CALL INPUT(X)

will be used by the main program to *obtain* a value for X to be used in later calculations.

We have so far used reading and writing operations in the examples, because the transmission of information between subroutine and main program in that case requires to be only in one direction. But the same subroutine can obtain a value from the main routine and return another value as well. For instance, a subsidiary calculation can be delegated to the subroutine as in the following:

    SUBROUTINE INVERT(A,B)
    B=1./A
    RETURN
    END

The CALL statement in the main program could be

    CALL INVERT(X,Y)

Here we introduce two parameters separated in the usual Fortran way by a comma. The first parameter is used to provide a value, in this case the value of X, to be used wherever A, the dummy first parameter, is mentioned in the subroutine. The second parameter is used to obtain the result from the subroutine, where it has been calculated under the pseudonym B. Notice at the machine level of detail, separate storage locations do not exist for A and B. They only show where to attach the addresses of the variable names specified in the CALL statement. The calculation actually performed in this example is

    Y=1./X

In this example the first parameter provides a value to the subroutine, the second returns a value to the main program. But they need not be in that order. As long as the parameters correspond properly both in the SUBROUTINE statement and the CALL statement, then they can be in any order.

Also, it is possible for the same parameter both to send and return a value. For instance

    SUBROUTINE INVERT(A)
    A=1./A
    RETURN
    END

can be called by

    CALL INVERT(X)

The value of X is taken from the main program, the inverse (one over it) is calculated and the result is returned as the value of X. As in any arithmetic calculation, the original value of X will have been destroyed.

Then again, more than one parameter can be used in this way. For example:

    SUBROUTINE SWAP(A,B)
    C=A
    A=B
    B=C
    RETURN
    END

which can be invoked by

    CALL SWAP(X,Y)

In this case, the values of main program variables X and Y are interchanged by the operation of the subroutine. Note in this case that the variable called C is not mentioned in the argument list, so it is entirely 'unknown' in the main program. The main program may use a variable named C but it will be stored and operated on entirely independently of the C in the subroutine. So as not to confuse things, we have used different variable names in the main program and subroutines, but we can choose any names we like, even the same ones, as long as they obey the Fortran naming conventions. Also, in the examples we have used only real variables. We can use integer names too as long as the *types* correspond in the list of parameters in the SUBROUTINE statement and the related CALL statements.

As is usual in Fortran, we may also write the name of an array wherever we have used a single variable, as long as the dimensions of corresponding arrays agree. If we used arrays in the subroutine however, they must be *separately* dimensioned in the subroutine (under the name used in the subroutine of course). For example:

```
      SUBROUTINE RAINU(A,B)
      DIMENSION A(20),B(20)
      DO 22 I=1,20
      B(I)=1./A(I)
   22 CONTINUE
      RETURN
      END
```

which can be invoked by

```
      CALL RAINU(X,Y)
```

where X and Y are also arrays of dimension 20 (declared in the main program). Notice that only the *names* of the arrays need be used in the parameter list.

Points to remember when using the parameter method of communication:

1. The number of parameters in the CALL statement and corresponding SUBROUTINE statement must be identical.
2. The parameters must correspond in type; a real variable in the CALL statement matching a real variable in the SUBROUTINE statement; and similarly for integers.
3. If a parameter is the name of a subscripted variable, a DIMENSION statement must appear in the subroutine declaring the size of the dummy parameter. The size of the dimension should be the same as the dimension assigned to the corresponding parameter in the routine containing the appropriate CALL statement.
4. Parameters in the CALL statement may be subscripted. The dummy parameters in the SUBROUTINE statement cannot be subscripted (they can though be the names of subscripted variables).

Example

10.1 Give an interpretation of the following program:

```
C       *** MAIN ROUTINE ***
        CALL IN(A,B,XY)
        CALL ARITH(A,B,XY,EQU)
        CALL OUT(EQU)
        STOP
        END
C
        SUBROUTINE IN(AA,BB,XYXY)
C       *** INPUT ROUTINE ***
        READ(5,333)AA,BB,XYXY
   333  FORMAT(1ØX,3F1Ø.4)
        RETURN
        END
C
        SUBROUTINE ARITH(A,B,XY,EQU)
C       *** ARITHMETIC ROUTINE ***
        EQU=A*XY+B
        RETURN
        END
C
        SUBROUTINE OUT(EQU)
C       *** OUTPUT ROUTINE ***
        WRITE(6,444)EQU
   444  FORMAT(1ØX,F1Ø.2)
        RETURN
        END
```

(Data as follows)
          9.6   1684.Ø   8.75Ø2

Notice that where successive items of data are punched in identical field widths the FORMAT statement explaining the layout of the data may use an abbreviated form, 3F10.4 instead of F10.4, F10.4, F10.4.

Program exercise 5

Write a program to read values into an array (ARRAY1) and then to transfer them to a second array (ARRAY2).
The program should consist of a main routine and a subroutine using parameters to enable communication between the two.
Make the main program responsible for the input of values to ARRAY1 and for printing out the contents of ARRAY2. Use SUBROUTINE COPY to transfer the values from one array to the other.
Data consists of real values to two decimal places with one value punched per card in positions 1-10. A final card is included which just has 999 punched in positions 11-13.
Structure the program to handle up to 10 data cards.

If you consider this exercise too straightforward on its own include a second subroutine to arrange the values in ascending order, storing them in ARRAY3, and write out the ordered list in the main routine.

11 Additional features

Communication between subprograms II

The second method of transferring data between subprograms involves the use of the COMMON statement. Usually the variables used in the main program and in each subroutine are kept in completely separate places in the computer store. If the value of a particular variable in the main program is required in a subroutine then, as we have seen, it may be mentioned as a parameter in a CALL statement and then the subroutine is 'told where it is'. This second method, in contrast, arranges that the main program and a subroutine can both have access to the same block of storage in a symmetrical way. For example, if we wish both the main program and subroutine to use three variables called A, B and C then the statement

        COMMON A, B, C

is placed at the head of the main program and also of the subroutine. When this is done, those three values are always available to both the main program and the subroutine.

To make this possible, the values corresponding to names mentioned in a COMMON statement are stored in a special *common storage area* and always strictly in the order in which they are named in the COMMON statement. In fact, wherever the COMMON statement occurs, in main program or subroutine, it is taken to *define* how the common storage area is laid out, starting from the first position.

This means practically that *all* the variables in the common area must be mentioned in *every* common statement. Otherwise we get problems such as the following:

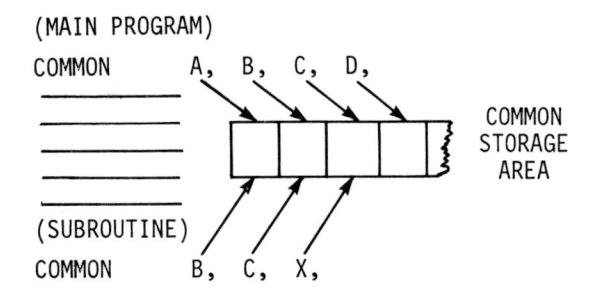

```
(MAIN PROGRAM)
COMMON      A,  B,  C,  D,
                                COMMON
                                STORAGE
                                AREA
(SUBROUTINE)
COMMON      B,  C,  X,
```

In this case the first position in the common storage area will be called A in the main program but will be called B in the subroutine; B in the main program will be called C in the subroutine, and so on.

This leads to the suggestion that *every* variable name used in the main and subprograms should be declared in *every* COMMON statement and then all the data can be shared freely. But the whole point of breaking a program into main and subprograms is that the component parts are separate and independent as far as possible so that writing and testing can proceed independently and program errors can quickly be traced to one particular subprogram. It is clear that data values worked on by each subprogram should also be kept separate as far as possible. So it is best to put in the COMMON statement only the names of variables which are to be shared. In any case the main program and each subroutine should carry identical COMMON statements.

The difference then between the use of the COMMON statement and the use of *parameters* is that with COMMON, the *same* name is normally used to refer to the common value in both main and subprogram, and all names shared by any subroutine must be mentioned in all of them, whereas with *parameters*, a *different* name for the same value is generally used in the CALL and SUBROUTINE statements, but only those variables shared by the main program and the *particular* subroutine need be mentioned.

The COMMON statement can also include array names together with their dimensions, for example:

    COMMON A, B(23), C(9,7)

When an array is mentioned in this way, it is not necessary to add a DIMENSION statement to specify the array size, since the necessary information is present already in the COMMON statement.

The replacement of variables by arithmetic expressions

In several of the statements described in previous chapters we have used a single variable where it is actually permitted to write an arithmetic expression. For example, in the CALL statement it is possible to replace any of the parameters which provide a value to the subroutine by an arithmetic expression. Consider the following subroutine:

    SUBROUTINE INVERT(A,B)
    B=1.0/A
    RETURN
    END

The corresponding CALL statement could be:

    CALL INVERT(X+2.0,Y)

The result of the call will be to give Y the value 1.0/(X+2.0) and the same is true of an expression involving any number of variables from the main program. As a special case, we can write a single constant into the call:

    CALL INVERT(2.0,Y)

will give Y the value 1.0/2.0.

On the surface this appears a valuable extra facility. But an equivalent effect to the two previous calls can be obtained by the following statements:

    V=X+2.0
    CALL INVERT(V,Y)

and

    V=2.0
    CALL INVERT(V,Y)

Also, when an arithmetic expression is being used in a CALL statement, extra considerations must be borne in mind to avoid error. In this particular example, the *second* parameter in the CALL statement cannot be replaced by an arithmetic expression, since it is providing a location to return a result. This may be easy to check, but if we consider a second example:

    SUBROUTINE INVERT(A)
    A=1.0/A
    RETURN
    END

it is easy to overlook that we are *not* allowed to write

    CALL INVERT(2.0)

since although the single parameter takes a value into the subroutine it also receives the result. In fact a call of this nature would probably have a most remarkable effect on the program. After the call had been executed, any following statements which used the constant 2.0 would find that it had been replaced by 1.0/2.0! There are also considerations of program management and efficiency which make it sensible to stick to the simple type of parameter.

Another example of 'complexification' occurs with the index of an array variable. It is possible to replace the K of A(K) with a simple form of arithmetic expression. Again, by the use of one extra assignment statement, we are able to replace K with anything we like,

so it seems pointless to try to remember the special forms of expression permitted in the
index position. In fact, if the same index is used in several places to select the particular member required it is more efficient to evaluate the expression in one position only
apart from being more readable, for example:

```
K=2*M+N+3
A(K)=B(K)+C(K)
```

However, the following forms of index can be used:

integer variable + *integer constant*	K+1
integer variable - *integer constant*	K-1
integer constant * *integer variable*	2*K
integer constant * *integer variable* + *integer constant*	2*K+1
integer constant * *integer variable* - *integer constant*	2*K-1

The implied DO loop
─────────────────

This feature of Fortran is directed towards economy in writing down statements. Consider
the requirement to read five values in a *single* data input record and to store them in five
positions in an array. Using the statements covered so far we may write

```
      READ(5,22)A(1),A(2),A(3),A(4),A(5)
   22 FORMAT(5F6.2)
```

But it is very easy to get this wrong. To minimize this problem, we can borrow a
principle from the DO statement, to control what is essentially a repetition with a changing
index.

```
      READ(5,22)(A(K),K=1,5)
```

The phrase in the second pair of brackets is a request to repeat A(K) with K taking the
values one to five in succession. Inside those brackets all the rules relevant in the
construction of the DO statement can be applied.
   A similar principle can be applied to write out a series of array members on a
line.

```
      WRITE(6,33)(A(K),K=1,5)
   33 FORMAT(1X,5F6.2)
```

Notice that this all has an entirely different effect from the use of an ordinary DO
loop. The sequence

```
      DO 22 K=1,5
      WRITE(6,33)A(K)
   33 FORMAT(1X,F6.2)
   22 CONTINUE
```

will print out *five* separate lines with one item on each.
   We may conveniently combine both of these facilities to read in or write out a two
dimensional array row by row as follows:

```
      DIMENSION A(5,8)
      DO 22 K=1,5
      READ(5,33)(A(K,N),N=1,8)
   33 FORMAT(8(4X,F6.2))
   22 CONTINUE
```

Notice in all these examples the presence of the comma in *front* of the 'loop counter' of
the implied DO. There is no comma in that position in the ordinary DO statement.

Format and the layout of results

So far, we have paid little attention to the way results are presented on the output page (or visual display unit). In fact, printing out a series of numerical values without any explanatory words surrounding them is not really helpful to anybody. An extra format facility opens up the possibility of understandable results.

Let us first consider the printing of a descriptive title for the results, such as "RESULTS FROM SPACE-PROBE".

This can be achieved in the following way:

    WRITE(6,33)
  33 FORMAT(1X,24HRESULTS FROM SPACE-PROBE)

The significant new part of the FORMAT statement is in the H in front of that which we require to be printed out. The figures in front of the H say how many characters following the H are to be printed out, in this case 24. Naturally the H itself is not printed out, it is a format code just like the X, I and F codes we have already seen. (H actually stands for Hollerith, who was a principal in the introduction of punched-card systems.)

Notice that the WRITE statement has no variable name attached to it since no *value* is being printed out.

It is possible to combine the printing-out of values and a suitable commentary in the same pair of instructions. For example if the current value of X is 357.9 then the statements

    WRITE(6,33)X
  33 FORMAT(1X,18HTHE VALUE OF X IS ,F5.1)

will print out

    THE VALUE OF X IS 357.9

Notice that we have included an extra space after the word "IS" so that the value of X is spaced out properly.

It is clear that a suitable combination of I, X, F, and H format codes will enable us to space out information on a line in any way we require. But what of the vertical spacing? Up to now, information has always been printed out on successive lines by the use of the 1X at the beginning of the FORMAT statement. Another awkward point of machine detail needs to be explained here.

When a line is to be printed, the sequence of characters representing that line is sent from storage to the printer. Conventionally, the first character to be sent is not actually printed, but serves to control the movement of the output paper in the vertical direction. The code employed in this first character position is as follows:

    the character 'blank'   print the present information on the next line to that which has just been printed (colloquially a 'line feed')

    the character '0'   print the present information on the next line but one (colloquially a 'line throw')

    the character '1'   print the present information on the first line of the next page (colloquially a 'page throw')

Now the significance of the 1X at the front of previous FORMAT statements can be seen; it specifies the first character in the output line as the blank character, which is interpreted as a request to move to the next line. We now have available another way of specifying the first character of the line, by using the H format code. For example:

    FORMAT(1H ,F6.3)

will have exactly the same effect as

    FORMAT(1X,F6.3)

for both provide this first blank character, whilst

    FORMAT(1H0,F6.3)

will provide a zero in the first character position which provides a 'line throw' on the printer, and

    FORMAT(1H1,F6.3)

will provide a one, to achieve a 'page throw' on the printer.
  Notice that none of these first control characters are ever printed out on a line, so the printed message actually starts with the second character in the FORMAT statement. The H format code can therefore do two different jobs, depending on its position in the FORMAT statement, and these jobs can be combined. For example, to write out RESULTS FROM SPACE-PROBE at the head of a new page, the FORMAT statement could be

    FORMAT(26H1 RESULTS FROM SPACE-PROBE)

  What if we require the next output line to be printed out several lines below the previous one? In this case Fortran uses yet another special format code, the slash or division symbol. When placed at a particular point in the FORMAT statement, it is just as if we had started a new FORMAT statement there *except* that it is still the same WRITE statement being obeyed. For example:

    WRITE(6,33)X,Y
  33 FORMAT(1X,F6.3/1X,F6.3)

will produce something like

    34.579
    23.685

  Notice that the first character after the slash is used as a vertical spacing code for the following line, just as at the beginning of the FORMAT statement. This leads to a slightly baffling but useful effect when we write several slashes together, for example:

    WRITE(6,33)X,Y
  33 FORMAT(1X,F6.3////1X,F6.3)

will produce the following output:

    34.579

    23.685

So *four* slashes produce *three* blank lines. The reason is that *between* each pair of slashes we have the equivalent of a *completely* blank line. But that includes a blank character as the first control character. So the printer moves the paper on to the next line. There are *three* blank lines between *four* slashes, and the final 1X moves the paper yet again so that the value for Y is printed on the fourth line below that for X.
  We now have sufficient facilities to lay out our results to any required level of elaboration.

Logical expressions

In the logical IF statement we have so far placed inside the brackets simple expressions of the type A.GT.B. These involve the relational operators *greater than*, *less than*, and so on. It is possible to write more complicated expressions which involve *logical* operators. For example, if we want the expression to be true whenever A is greater than B and at the same time C is greater than D we can write

    IF(A.GT.B.AND.C.GT.D)

  If we want the expression to be true whenever A is greater than B *or* C is greater than D (not necessarily both) then we can write

    IF(A.GT.B.OR.C.GT.D)

  If we want to *reverse* the effect of one of the relational expressions, for example the total expression is to be true when A is greater than B and also it is not true that C is greater than D, then we can write:

    IF(A.GT.B.AND..NOT.C.GT.D)

So the three logical operators .AND. .OR. and .NOT. can be used to build up complicated expressions as required. This enables us to write rather natural looking expressions like

    IF(HEIGHT.GT.6.2.AND.WEIGHT.GT.227.0)

Two points need watching carefully however. At a detailed level, there are a great number of full stops to get in exactly the right positions. At a more general level, the meanings of .AND. .OR. and .NOT. are very precise and a normal rather vague use of these words in a problem solution will have to be tightened up considerably before it can be put into a program.

It is also possible to include arithmetic expressions within logical expressions. For example we can write

    IF(A.GT.B*C)

though the advantage of this is doubtful for we can achieve the same end with greater clarity by writing

    X=B*C
    IF(A.GT.X)

The following table shows the order in which operators are evaluated where logical expressions are in use.

Level 1	subexpressions contained in brackets
Level 2	exponentiation (raising to a power)
Level 3	multiplication, division
Level 4	addition, subtraction
Level 5	.EQ. .NE. .LT. .LE. .GT. .GE.
Level 6	.NOT.
Level 7	.AND.
Level 8	.OR.

Library functions

The subroutine facility enables us to write any required subprogram as a separate entity. We may find that once a particular subroutine has been written, it can be used by several of our main programs. So we can start to build up a library of useful subroutines, which can be co-ordinated by a suitable main program, and therefore save much effort in continually constructing programs from scratch. Some subprograms, particularly in numerical computation, are so often required by many different computer users, that Fortran provides a ready-written collection of these which can be assumed to be available. It is necessary only to call them into operation when they are required. Many of these *library* subprograms are so elementary that it is convenient to have an even simpler method than the use of the CALL statement to initiate them. For example, a subprogram which takes the square root of some real number is usually required in the evaluation of an arithmetic expression, so Fortran provides a means of requesting that subprogram *during* the evaluation of the expression. The assignment statement

    X=A+SQRT(Y)

is evaluated in the following way. The right-hand side of the assignment consists of a variable named A to be added to something which looks like a member of an array, though it has the wrong sort of variable as its index. The library is then checked and it is found that there is a subprogram called SQRT (short for square root) already in existence. This subprogram is then brought into action, with the value inside the brackets used as a parameter. In this, this particular subprogram will evaluate the square root of the variable called Y. This result is then made available as the *value* of SQRT(Y) at that particular position in the arithmetic expression. Therefore it is added to the value of A and the sum is assigned as the value of X. A selected list of such *library functions* is given overleaf. Several of the functions normally available require more than one parameter, but these are used only to provide values *to* the subprogram. The only result which comes out through the operation of the subprogram is its *value* which is used in evaluating the corresponding arithmetic expression.

It is also possible to nest a function within a function in a single assignment statement as for example:

    A=SQRT(1.0-SIN(X)*SIN(X))

which is evaluated in the following way. The library is checked and it is found that there is a subprogram called SIN (short for sine) already in existence. This subprogram is brought into action, evaluating the sine of the variable called X. This result is then squared and subtracted from 1.0 to provide the parameter for the square root function. The subprogram is then brought into play, evaluated and the result assigned to A.

Here is a selection of the available library routines:

Name	Parameter	Result	Definition
SQRT	real	real	square root
TAN	real	real	tangent
SIN	real	real	sine
COS	real	real	cosine
EXP	real	real	exponential
ALOG	real	real	natural log
ALOG10	real	real	common log
ABS	real	real	absolute value (real values)
IABS	integer	integer	absolute value (integer values)
FLOAT	integer	real	conversion (integer to real)
IFIX	real	integer	conversion (real to integer)
AMAX1	real (2 or more)	real	largest value (reals)
MAX0	integer (2 or more)	integer	largest value (integers)
AMIN1	real (2 or more)	real	smallest value (reals)
MIN0	integer (2 or more)	integer	smallest value (integers)

Examples

11.1 Write a sequence of statements which assign six elements to an array called A.

11.2 Assuming you have just read 50 values into an array AR, made up of 10 rows by 5 columns, described by DIMENSION AR(10,5), now write down the statements necessary to write out all 50 values, row by row, using both an implied DO loop and an ordinary DO loop.

11.3 Describe the layout of the output produced by the following statements:

        WRITE(6,12)A,B
     12 FORMAT(1H1,F10.4/////1X,F10.4)

11.4 Other than the number of statements required, what is the difference between the following two sequences?

        DO 10 K=1,5
        READ(5,20)A(K)
     20 FORMAT(F7.3)
     10 CONTINUE

        READ(5,10)(A(K),K=1,5)
     10 FORMAT(5F7.3)

11.5 Write a Fortran statement to test the condition that X is larger than Y as well as A larger than C.

11.6 Write down the statements necessary to interchange the row and column values of a two-dimensional ten by ten array A without losing any values.

11.7 Write a program to read in a set of numbers and to sort and print them out in ascending order. There are 80 numbers and 8 values of F10.4 format punched per data card.

12 Programming quality

The objective of the previous chapters is to introduce a basic programming method, and they can be covered in a few tens of hours of study and practice. Learning to write *good* programs is altogether a different matter and is likely to take much longer. Essentially it is a matter of effective resource management where the principal resources involved are the time spent by the programmer in developing and maintaining the program and the computing resources involved in developing, testing and producing useful results over the 'life cycle' of the program.

Stages of program development

Let us consider the life-cycle of a program in more detail. The programming process can be defined in five stages; problem analysis, program design, program construction, a consolidation phase of testing, correcting and improving and finally a maintenance phase which lasts until the program is not used further.

Problem analysis is completed when we have a clear definition of the problem to be solved. It is really a definition of the *output* required in terms of the *input* available and so it is a definition of the relevant *data structures*. *Program design* is a continuation of the analysis with the addition of the *constraints* imposed by the use of computers. The structure of the input will be constrained by the way it is obtained and also by the way in which it is to be taken into the program. These considerations will lead to the design of a suitable structure for the input record.

The form of the output will be constrained by the output device and the user's requirements, leading to the design of a suitable output layout. The general design of the program will be constrained by the availability of hardware and software, the existence of relevant algorithms and program libraries and the availability of compilers for a particular programming language. Each constraint involves a design choice which is also governed by assumptions such as the continued existence of a machine or a programming language. The design choice is also governed by the individual's design philosophy, concerning such things as safety factors and the time, space and programming resources likely to be available. The actual process of design is not directly definable except in that it produces a plan for creating the output from a specified input subject to the design constraints.

After program design comes *program construction*, which is really a specification of the design at a level at which it can be directly interpreted by the computing system.

After the program has been constructed, it is the experience of most programmers that we are brought into unpleasant contact with the real world. That is, the program does not perform as it should. At first, it may refuse to perform at all, due to the presence of errors in the specification of the program statements. Once these have been overcome, it will be provided with test input data. The test data will no doubt demonstrate that the program does not correspond precisely enough with the original design plan, and we will enter a phase where a sequence of (hopefully) minor adjustments are made to the design and resulting construction of the program to bring it into line with requirements. The testing procedure will gradually progress from employing small amounts of data where the results to be expected are already known, up to sample runs on 'real-life' data which are designed to test the program very comprehensively in all its parts.

Finally, the program is unleashed on real data and the struggle to maintain it in operation through changing data, changing compilers, changing operating systems and changing computing systems is commenced.

Program qualities

We suggest that a good program will have qualities which make it easy to develop, test and run to produce results over an extensive life-cycle. So, what are these qualities?

We can consider program qualities in two groups, those which contribute to immediate use, and those which lead to a long life for the program. Under immediate qualities we can first suggest correctness, that is, the program should do the job it was designed for. Correctness is easy to request but very difficult to ensure. When we first have the idea for a program it is naturally vague and imprecise. Gradually a firmer definition of the job to be done emerges as we refine the program plan. It is useful to return and reconsider the original objectives at every stage of the refinement, especially where it has been necessary to rearrange the original plan because of hardware, operating system or programming language constraints. It is very easy to confuse logical correctness of program structure, which we can achieve, with a precise fit to the original requirements, of which we can *never* be certain.

Another property which is easy to specify but difficult to ensure is *robustness*. The program should accept a wide range of inputs and in particular should not 'blow up' in an indeterminate manner when presented with data which is not to the correct specification. This involves much consideration of the expected range of input data values and a comprehensive battery of checks to ensure that unacceptable values do not cause chaos in later arithmetic, such as initiating division by zero.

Again, the program should be *easy to use*. Data should not have to be specified in very precise and complicated formats. It should not be necessary to provide long strings of numerical parameters to achieve specific options. The character-processing techniques shown at the end of chapter 13 can be helpful here.

The final immediately useful quality is *efficiency*. It is important here to be very sure of what we mean. In the past, many programmers have wasted a great deal of *human* resource in trying to save a comparatively insignificant amount of *machine* resource. It is likely that economies arising from an improved overall *design* will far outweigh those produced by adjusting existing programs at a detailed level. In particular, the use of 'clever tricks' to increase efficiency will almost certainly decrease some of the other program qualities we consider next.

The second of the two groups of program qualities is those concerned with program *endurance*, that is, the ability of a program to continue to be used for a long time. These qualities are all connected with the ability to tolerate changes in the working environment.

Reliability is the long-term aspect of correctness. The changes being tolerated by a reliable program will include different types of data and variations in the method of use of the program which were built into the design but have perhaps not been exercised previously. The reliability of a program will be probed by comprehensive testing procedures, but it is important to note that programs can be *proved* only to be unreliable. In the real world of practical computer operation there is no such thing as perfection, however hard we may try to achieve it, and design and testing procedures must be seen as limited resources which provide limited returns.

However well designed the program, there will be changes in the operating systems and hardware which necessitate minor modifications to keep it running. A good program will be easily *maintainable* under these conditions; it will require minimum modification and it will be easy to carry out the necessary modifications. More serious changes in the program environment will come from a complete change of computer and operating system. We require the program to be *portable*, so it will continue to do the same thing in a different location hopefully doing useful work for someone else as well as the originator. The most thorough-going change in environment is the requirement that the program should do something *different* to a greater or lesser extent. A good program can even help in this situation by being easily *modifiable*.

In general, the key to endurance is the provision of simple, well-defined interfaces between the program and its working environment and between subsections of the program. The program should depend on the minimum features special to a particular operating system and it should accept data in one of the standard coded formats approved for interchange between computing systems. Notice that these features may well be opposed to execution efficiency. Concerning subsections of the program, the essence of modifiability is the *modularity* of the program such that the separate modules can be easily rearranged and added to in order to meet new requirements. In particular, those parts of the program which depend on particular features of the operating system such as obtaining data from a special storage device should be separated, so that it is clear which parts of the program require to be modified when the operating system changes.

A final program quality is concerned with both current and future effectiveness. This is *understandability*, since the programmer needs to be constantly reminded of the way the program works *and* why it is that way, both during program construction and particularly when modifications become necessary. Understanding is closely related to documentation and will be discussed further at the end of the chapter.

Program design

A good programmer will produce good programs quickly, with the minimum use of computing resources. Is there a program development method which can be followed to ensure success?

Many design methods have been proposed during the last ten years and unfortunately several have been championed and elaborated to the level of a cult, guaranteeing success in programming for those who follow the rules. Unfortunately, programming is very much a personal activity, and while certain overall principles can be helpful, each successful programmer will develop a method which optimizes on their particular skills and fits their particular constraints. In Chapter 3 we introduced the idea of a program plan to assist in program development. The design method inherent in the program plan can be summarised in a series of principles.

The main principle is "divide and conquer". That is, a large problem is subdivided into a series of smaller problems which are kept as separate from each other as possible. If this process is repeated on each subproblem then the description of the problem becomes a hierarchy of descriptions of subproblems. If we continue far enough in this splitting up process then we eventually get the resulting subproblems down to a size and complexity which we can solve directly. The solutions to the separate subproblems can then be re-combined in the pattern of the original hierarchy to produce an overall solution to the original problem.

The second principle is that the final program structure is most easily developed if it corresponds to the hierarchic structure of the original problem, as it has been thought out by the programmer. That is, the solution to each *subproblem* is coded as a separate *subprogram* and these are combined in groups, with a 'higher-level' subprogram merely initiating a group of subprograms 'lower' than itself in the hierarchy. The main program is then in its turn merely a sequence of initiations of the subprograms at the next level down in the hierarchy. By 'initiation' we mean 'providing with data and setting in motion'.

The third principle concerns trying to apply the first and second principles to the *data* as well as the *program*. Roughly, we try to establish a relationship between program and data such that a particular part of the program deals with a particular part of the data. In a hierarchically planned program this presupposes that the structure of the program is mirrored in a hierarchic structuring of the data. If the data has already been organized in a particular way, perhaps for use with other programs, then this implies that the structure of the new program should be based on the existing structure of the data. Naturally this is only relevant where some sort of hierarchic structure can be imposed on the data, such as where the data concerns the parts which go to make up a piece of industrial equipment.

The final principle is really only a corollary of the first. If we solve a problem by splitting it up into a hierarchy of subproblems, this presupposes that we start with an overall view of the problem and we *successively refine* our idea of what the problem *is* as we split it into smaller subproblems. This implies in turn that we defer the consideration of details as long as possible. In particular, we do not attempt to write pieces of program until the problem hierarchy, and therefore the solution hierarchy, has been established. Not until then can we know exactly what a particular part of the program is to do and how it is to be related to other parts of the program.

The hierarchy of solution can be planned out on paper, with the aid of the informal bracketing arrangement we introduced in Chapter 3. There, the brackets enclosed groups of statements which were intimately related to each other, such as what happens if the answer to a question is YES or a sequence which is to be repeated several times. These groups can be seen as the lowest levels of a more comprehensive hierarchy which represents the process of successive refinement of objectives as we move from a general statement of the solution to a particular specification of the solution. On the left-hand side of the program plan we have a single bracket which represents the total solution. Immediately inside we have a sequence of brackets which represent subsolutions. There may be several levels of these representing successive refinements of the subsolutions, and then we reach a sequence of brackets which represents the individual subroutines at the lowest level of the hierarchy. After that we have the last few levels of detailed program plan representing how each subroutine is realised and finally the equivalent sequence in the chosen programming language on the right-hand side of the program plan.

This description of the program plan represents a very much idealised view of program development. In practice we do not progress smoothly from the general to the particular and there will be many false starts and redrawings of the plan as we take into account the design constraints imposed by a particular operating system and programming language. Again, the hierarchic structure will not necessarily be pure in the sense that successive refinements of the problem move sweetly into matching subroutines of the solution. Many problems, especially the large, difficult ones with no obvious structure in the data may refuse to be split down into any obvious hierarchy of self-contained subproblems at all. We must remember that the hierarchic structure is a convenient way of representing a *model* of a real situation in our minds and that there is no *necessity* for there to exist a nice, simple, and clean solution to any problem 'out there' in the real world.

Programming for quality

Now let us consider some more detailed techniques of program construction which can contribute to program quality.

The basic rule is to aim for simplicity and do things in an obvious way. As we have stated before, 'cunning' programming, which exploits certain esoteric properties of the computer or the programming language, is very difficult to get right and the time spent in writing clever programs is rarely justified. Usually this results from an attempt to minimize a particular resource, say execution time, while neglecting the much greater use of programmer resource in developing and maintaining such a tricky program. With the continual decrease in hardware costs relative to software production costs this becomes more and more wasteful of total resource. Again, it is not necessary to use statements up to the limit of their inherent complexity. A rather larger number of simpler statements is probably easier to check and get right.

The understandability of a Fortran program is very much connected with variable names, statement numbers, and the use of storage. *Variable names* are most helpful if they *mean* something, that is, they describe the data values which they represent. We have used names such as A, I and X for brevity in the examples but they may well be replaced by such as HEIGHT and TIME in practical programs. Of course, A, I and X may be relevant to the mathematical description of a particular method as it is realized in a generalized subroutine. It is best not to mix numeric and alphabetic characters in variable names: in fact, it is best to avoid using letters which can be mistaken for numbers and vice versa whenever possible. This concerns Ø and O, 1 and I, 2 and Z, 5 and S in particular.

Statement numbers provide a fertile field for mistakes. Many programmers use different groups of numbers according to their use, for example two digit numbers for the destination of GO TO statements, three digit numbers for DO statements, four digit numbers for FORMAT. Others use consecutive numbers in strict sequence through the program. It is essential to use some organized way of assigning statement numbers, otherwise the universal law will ensure that a number is erroneously duplicated very soon.

The organization and naming of data provides some subtle problems. For maximum independence of subroutines it is best to avoid the use of COMMON as far as possible and employ parameters for the explicit transfer of information between subroutines. Many complain that this forces the use of too many parameters and therefore leads to errors in CALL and SUBROUTINE statements. Perhaps the criterion for a useful subroutine is that it *can* be specified with a realistic number of parameters. Difficulties of this kind lead to the concept of a data *workspace* consisting of a single array whose individual components have well-defined purposes and comprise *all* the information which is required to be shared between subroutines. This space is strictly limited and all the routines are designed to use it in a disciplined manner. The same design of workspace may then be used by many different programs and may be permitted to be declared as the only component of COMMON.

Another important component of understandability is the *readability* of a listed program. The rules of Fortran allow any number of spaces to be interspersed between other characters except when using the H format. This can be used to make statements more readable, for example by putting a space on each side of an equals sign, but this should not be overdone. Separate groups of statements such as repetition sections may be indented a certain number of spaces to the right as in some of the examples. Considerable improvements in clarity come from the use of comment cards to separate individual sections of program such as:

```
        _____
        _____
        _____
C
C       *************
C
        _____
        _____
        _____
```

In fact, any way of laying out the program so that it reflects the arrangement of the program plan will be helpful.

Now let us consider program aids to help during correcting, testing and practical use. There are two general principles to help us. The first is that a good program is defensively coded, the second, that it is talkative. *Defensive coding* refers to the insertion of a large variety of checks to ensure that the program is proceeding as expected. For example, data is checked for acceptability when it enters the program and before every sensitive calculation. The acceptability of data values is usually defined in terms of a range of possible values and a sequence such as the following can be used frequently.

```
      IF(X.GT.0.1.AND.X.LT.9.99)GO TO 22
      WRITE(6,33)X
   33 FORMAT(30H X IS OUTSIDE LIMITS,VALUE IS ,F6.2)
      STOP
   22 CONTINUE
```

Since attempted division by zero is such a common error it is useful to check the value of every divisor. Another common error, concerning the indices of arrays getting out of bounds can be tested for in a similar way.

By a *talkative* program we mean one which reports continuously on its output how the computation is proceeding and so provides valuable aids to pinpointing errors in addition to error messages from the operating system. This can be achieved by a copious supply of WRITE statements such as the following:

```
      WRITE(6,33)X
   33 FORMAT(36H ENTERED SUBROUTINE A,VALUE OF X IS ,F6.2)
```

When these statements have done their job, we can simply 'comment them out' by inserting a C in their first character position. It is best not to remove them completely, since they may well prove useful again when the program is modified. If there are several possible correct stopping positions for a program it is useful to indicate which one has occurred by a similar report.

Concerning errors in general, the user is warned against low-level error correction, that is, the use of various aids provided by most operating systems for the use of full-time professional systems programmers. These include such things as the printing out of the value in each storage location at the termination of an incorrect program. They require a considerable knowledge of a specific computing system and come from the time when the user and the engineer building the computer were one and the same person. Let the professional advisors use them if they wish in assisting you!

Many of the previous points on program construction reflect the necessity to write into a program aids to testing and correcting, on the *assumption* that something will go wrong at some time, which is a basic fact of experience. Most of these errors are due to the unexpected consequences of particular patterns of data or of attempted use and cannot be predicted or tested for exhaustively in advance. Any newly-completed program will have in addition syntax errors in the construction of program statements and rather straight-forward mistakes in the implementation of the program plan such that, for example, a repetition takes place too many times.

Syntax errors can be reduced in frequency by learning to *read* programs rather than merely writing them. In other words, a calm and critical examination of the code *before* it is submitted for execution is far more effective in saving overall time than a frantic check through a program when you have already wasted too much time by submitting it with errors in the first place. It may seem helpful to let the compiler sort out the syntax errors but this attitude can too easily extend to a lack of care at all stages of program development, and a complete failure to produce a working program in the required time-scale.

Testing by hand

Simple errors in the program plan implementation can often be discovered by *hand testing* sections of the program in a very simple way. The programmer makes up a suitable small selection of the test data which is required by the program and then *simulates* the action of the computer by obeying the sequence of instructions and writing down the resulting values of the variables involved. For example, consider a section of the code which is supposed to read a sequence of five values into an array A.

```
      K=1
   22 CONTINUE
      IF(K.GT.6)GO TO 33
      READ(5,32)A(K)
      K=K+1
      GO TO 22
   33 CONTINUE
```

The programmer knows that a sequence of five values is expected, so invents them;

```
5.2
7.9
8.6
3.2
4.7
```

and simulates the program with the aid of a sequence chart. The variables mentioned in the program are written down in sequence as they occur and are assigned the values indicated opposite them exactly as the program specifies. As a new value is assigned to a variable, the previous value is crossed out and the new value written down on the chart. In this example we first encounter

    K=1

so we write down

```
K | 1
```

and obey the following instructions with the given value of K. Let us represent what the programmer does as a 'stream of consciousness'.

"Continue – is K greater than six? – no, so go on to next instruction – read a value into A(1) so add to the chart."

```
   K  | 1
A(1)  | 5.2
```

"K equals K plus one, so K is two, modify the chart."

```
   K  | 1̸ 2
A(1)  | 5.2
```

"Go to 22. Is K greater than six? – no, so go to the next instruction – read the next value into A(2) and add to the chart."

```
   K  | 1̸ 2
A(1)  | 5.2
A(2)  | 7.9
```

This process is continued until we are satisfied that things are going well. In this particular example we will discover that we have been requested to read a value into A(6) and there is no corresponding value to read in. The logical IF has clearly been specified incorrectly and can be corrected straight away. The value of this method may not be clear from the very simple example demonstrated but it can be really helpful in connection with more complicated sequences.

The emphasis laid on *defensive programming* in this coverage of program construction clearly leads to a rule which governs the employment of all results: NEVER TRUST RESULTS WHICH COME FROM A COMPUTER. It is only too easy to confuse quantity with quality, but remember that the results can only be as good as the algorithm by which they are produced. It may even be worth considering the writing of *two* programs to produce the required results if they are critically important, and they can then be checked against each other for consistency.

Finally, a word on two topics which are intimately connected with the endurance of a program, the use of standard programming language features and the provision of documentation.

Programming language standards

Users of any computing installation will soon become aware that any Fortran compiler which they use provides a great number of alternative statement forms which have not been described in previous chapters. Some of these belong to *Standard Fortran*. Since 1966 there has been in existence a standard definition of the Fortran language, and a selective summary of the statements defined there will be carried out in the next chapter. Many statement forms are non-standard. They have been added to a particular compiler by their authors because they were thought to extend the power or improve the quality of *Standard Fortran*. Such additions are well meant, but dangerous to use. Since they occur on a particular compiler only, they *ensure* that a program using them will *not* be directly transferable to another compiler or computing system. They are also likely to be less understood by programming advisors and naturally, will not be explained in any of the standard texts. Their use fits into the category of clever programming and is not recommended.

Since 1966, a great deal of thought and discussion has been devoted to the subject of program language design, and many would say that Fortran has now been made obsolete unless it is able to incorporate improved design features. As a result, a new standard for Fortran is being published at the present time.

Unfortunately, the value of a programming language standard lies not in its beauty or its comprehensiveness, or its power to please anybody in particular, but in its ability to enable programs written to that standard to be understood and used in many places and for as long as possible. This implies that a standard may be added to but not reduced if it is not to lose its value for all those programs previously written. In the main the new standard includes the old standard, and it is certain that those parts not included will be incorporated for safety in every significant compiler. That is, we can continue to work with the old standard until the new standard has proved its worth. In fact, we consider that the new standard is not helpful since it does not go far enough in incorporating a consistent collection of statements of improved design which can be taught as a better basis of programming, while it goes too far in incorporating a large number of new features which will greatly increase the size of the compiler and will be difficult to incorporate consistently in a wide variety of operating systems. On the contrary, we would recommend that programmers adopt for themselves a subset of the 1966 standard which will guarantee transferability for a long time to come. For those who wish to consider the situation further, the book by Colin Day given in the list of references surveys the standard situation and provides a consistent subset. Our views on Fortran use are presented in more detail in the next chapter.

The importance of documentation

The value of *documentation* as an aid to understanding programs and therefore enabling them to be used and modified has not been mentioned earlier because of the danger of confirming the commonly-held impression that documentation occurs as a *stage* of program production, such as writing down what has been done after it has been completed. In fact if it is treated as such it will almost certainly fail in its true purpose. Documentation can be defined as the totality of information required to bring a program into use. This includes the original rough notes of the problem analysis, all the information inherent in the program plan, the program itself, instructions for using it, test data and results of test runs. If well designed, the code in itself can provide a considerable amount of explanation, but it is confined by the nature of current programming languages to a specific level of detail. Since people work in 'hierarchies of understanding' it is necessary to supplement the code with higher-level descriptions which are naturally in a native language. These may be *in-line* in the form of comments in the program or provided as separate documents. In any case they represent an integral part of the design of the program as a process of successive refinement. They are written *first* and the program statements follow after. They are primarily for the use of the person creating the program and only later are they used as an aid in transferring the program to another user and/or another machine.

In this short summary of programming techniques we have clearly had to gloss over a great number of important points. Some additional techniques depending on the processing of individual characters are covered in the next chapter but for an adequate summary of the field we must refer the reader to more specialised texts which are mentioned in chapter fourteen.

13 A survey of Fortran

The previous twelve chapters are what we believe to be the right amount of material for a first course in programming. With the aid of these Fortran features already described it is possible to construct a wide range of useful programs. We have purposely not aimed at an exhaustive description of each feature because we know that this is merely confusing for those who are just beginning to program. However, it is natural for all of us to want to explore beyond any boundaries which have been laid down and in this chapter we will attempt a more complete survey of the Fortran language, building on what has been already used.

Straightaway it should be stressed that knowledge of more *advanced* features in a programming language does not necessarily lead to the construction of *better* programs. In the previous chapter we have stressed the importance of simplicity in programming, and the experienced programmer does not use additional or more complicated forms of instruction unless they are essential in order to express the program in a simpler way *overall*. The wider the range of statement types used, the wider is the range of possible errors. What follows is an evaluative review of the *use* of Fortran statements rather than a totally comprehensive reference manual and this will naturally reflect a personal viewpoint. For those who desire completeness there is an unlimited number of books which cover Fortran in an exhaustive manner.

In this chapter we will first look at the related families of statement types which comprise Fortran and then look at each family in turn.

Families of statements

We can consider six families of statements in Fortran.

First, we require to define the data objects which are to be processed in the program, how big they are and what type. Previously we have defined *real* and *integer* numbers *implicitly*, but we will see that explicit definition using the words REAL and INTEGER is possible. Another object which we process is an *array* and this is defined in a way by the use of the DIMENSION statement, though this could be said to belong to the next family as well.

Second, we specify how the data objects are to be stored. We have already met DIMENSION and COMMON which are relevant here.

Third is calculation and assignment to storage. The familiar assignment statement does both, since calculation is specified on the right-hand side of the equals sign, while a value is assigned to a particular location in storage through something written to the left-hand side of the equals sign.

The fourth family is concerned with input and output. We have already met READ and WRITE and FORMAT.

The fifth family controls the flow of the program, that is, the order in which statements are performed. The logical IF, DO, CALL, RETURN and STOP belong to this group.

Finally, there are the statements which give structure and organisation to the program as it is written down. SUBROUTINE and END belong to this family.

These groupings are only suggested to help arrange the statements in the user's memory since several statements will be found to stray over the family boundaries. We will try to illustrate the effective use of each statement and point out the problems which may arise in practical use.

Data objects

So far, we have encountered two sorts of data, single valued variables and arrays, that is, indexed collections of variables. Both of these can be of real or integer type. It has been necessary to inform the compiler of the dimensions of arrays, since the correct number of storage spaces could not be set aside otherwise. However, this single variable has not been announced in any way. Storage space has been allocated simply through using a particular variable name somewhere in the program. Such a method of definition is called *implicit*. Whether the variable value is real or integer is determined by the Fortran naming convention. But another method is permitted. It is possible to write at the beginning of a program an *explicit* declaration such as:

```
      REAL I,J,K
      INTEGER A,B,C,D
```

Here the implicit naming convention has been overruled and I,J,K are *real* variables while A,B,C and D are *integers*. All other variable names not mentioned in the explicit declarations follow the *implicit* convention. This seems useful where the natural name for a variable is of the wrong implicit type. But there are other considerations as well.

Many other programming languages have only the *explicit* convention and many writers suggest that it is good programming practice to declare *all* variable names at the head of each program and subprogram in any case. These other languages often have a richer selection of possibilities than real and integer and it may well be a good suggestion if this is the case. In fact, Fortran itself has a richer variety than REAL and INTEGER but we have chosen not to introduce them because we believe the added complexity in defining and using these extra types is not justified in terms of extra program power or clarity. We suggest that all variable names and their types *should* be at the head of each subprogram in the form of a long comment, which will then include higher-level information about the meaning and use of each variable. Some may like to declare them all explicitly as well.

Arrays can also be defined explicitly.

```
      REAL A(25),K(25)
```

replaces

```
      DIMENSION A(25),K(25)
```

and also overrides the implicit naming convention.

A final point: if *all* variables are defined implicitly then any particular statement can be checked directly for compatible types *without* reference to a possible rather long and tedious definition at the head of the program. Some claim that this outweighs any other convenience of explicit types.

The storage of data

We have seen previously that the data type declarations of the form REAL A and INTEGER A, although determining the way in which the corresponding values are to be involved in calculations also imply how the values are to be stored. If variable names occur in the program without an explicit type definition then space will be set aside for the corresponding value in storage as implied by the name. Since an array *size* cannot be implicit, the DIMENSION statement must be used to specify the storage space required by the array, although the *type* of values being stored is defined *implicitly*. Statements like INTEGER A(22,22) define both the type *and* the array dimensions explicitly and a corresponding DIMENSION statement is not required.

The other statements dealt with here are concerned with the *sharing* of storage either by variables in different subprograms or by different variables in the *same* subprogram. In either case this results in being able to specify operations on the *same* piece of data by using *different* names for it, with all the related dangers of being unable to trace what has happened when something goes wrong, so this can be justified only in certain special cases which will be described.

The COMMON statement

As we have seen already, the COMMON statement is used so that data values may be shared between subprograms. The COMMON statement demonstrated already defines a single area in storage which *all* subprograms can reach and access is gained by putting a suitable COMMON statement in the subprogram which requires to reach that area. As we saw, the values in COMMON are shared not through using the same *names* but by defining in *every* COMMON statement what each storage location starting from the first will be called in that particular subprogram.

To reduce the danger of having a storage area that could be tampered with by *every* subprogram it is possible to set aside separate storage areas which can be shared by particular different groups of subprograms independently. This is called *labelled* COMMON because the separate COMMON areas are given names or *labels*, for example:

```
      SUBROUTINE SUBA
      COMMON/A/X,Y,Z
      _____
      _____
      END
      SUBROUTINE SUBB
      COMMON/A/X,Y,Z
      _____
      _____
      END
```

Here we have created a labelled COMMON block of storage which we have called A, and both subroutines have access to that block. The name of the block is enclosed between slashes immediately after the word COMMON and is followed by the names of the variables to which that block is given, starting from the first position. If we had written

```
      COMMON/A/T,W,G
```

in the second subroutine then T would refer to the same location as X in the first subroutine and so on.

The block name A can be replaced by any permitted Fortran name, and real and integer considerations are not relevant.

The type of common block used previously is distinguished from labelled COMMON by calling it *blank* or *unlabelled* COMMON. The difference lies simply in omitting the name and accompanying slashes completely, as used previously, or just the name, as in

```
      COMMON//X,Y,Z
```

where there is nothing between the slashes and X,Y,Z are stored in the first three locations of the single *blank COMMON* area.

A very careful check must be kept on the contents of the various COMMON blocks, since unexpected alterations to values in COMMON storage through errors in a subroutine apparently unconnected with that one under suspicion provide some of the most difficult problems in program correction. It is suggested that a program which must use COMMON storage should use labelled COMMON only, and should define *all* the labelled blocks in separate statements at the head of the main program as follows:

```
      COMMON/BLOCK1/A,B,C,D
      COMMON/BLOCK2/E,F
      COMMON/BLOCK3/G,H,K
```

Identical copies of these statements are placed at the heads of the relevant subroutines. This rule needs countermanding only when COMMON storage requirements are so large that certain advantages in storage efficiency require the use of blank COMMON. In this case specialist advice should be obtained.

Calculation and assignment
──────────────────────────

Arithmetic calculations in Fortran are specified on the right-hand side of an assignment statement as is already very familiar. The restriction to integers or real values but not both on the right-hand side may appear irksome, and many compilers allow this convention to be relaxed. However, since real and integer values are stored in fundamentally different ways, it is necessary for the compiler to apply an elaborate set of combination rules when they are used together and we believe it is better for the programmer to carry out explicit type conversions to one or the other type when they are to be combined since the representation and very likely the *precision* is going to be changed at that point. Previously, we have suggested type conversion through reassignment to a variable name of the opposite type, such as:

```
      A=I
```

Now we suggest that it is better to use the standard library functions

```
      A=FLOAT(I)
```

and

```
      I=IFIX(A)
```

to make it totally obvious that a conversion is taking place. These functions can also be used directly in an arithmetic expression and so extra statements are not necessary, for example:

    Z=B+FLOAT(K)

performs real arithmetic, while

    M=IFIX(B)-K

will be carried out in integer arithmetic.

Concerning the assignment of a value to a particular variable we have in addition to the familiar assignment statement another method involving the DATA statement, for example:

    DATA X/1.5176/

results in the assignment of the value 1.5176 to the variable X. The constant value to be assigned is enclosed by slashes and should naturally be of the same type as the named variable.

It may appear that the statement: X=1.5176 should produce exactly the same effect. However, the DATA statement results in X receiving the value 1.5176 during compilation time while the assignment statement results in the value being put in during execution, which takes up time and space for the instructions to do it. The value in X can be altered later in the program, but its usual job is to provide constants to the program.

We can extend this in the usual way to assign values to several variables, for example:

    DATA X,Y,Z/2.3,3.4,4.5/

gives the value 2.3 to X, 3.4 to Y and 4.5 to Z. Notice that the values as well as the variable names are separated by commas.

Program flow
─────────────

In this group of statements for controlling the order in which other statements are executed we have: CONTINUE, logical IF, GO TO, STOP, DO, CALL and RETURN. Although there are several others in standard Fortran, we do not recommend their use.

Although CONTINUE does nothing except transfer control to the following instruction, we have already pointed out its value as the natural 'place-holder' for a statement number, particularly at the end of a DO loop. We would like to extend this principle and suggest that all statement numbers connected with the flow of control during execution are attached to CONTINUE statements only. The CONTINUE statement will then serve as a clear marker for the beginning (or in the case of the DO loop, the end) of a block of code which is to be obeyed sequentially. These blocks will naturally be described by a single phrase in a higher level of the program plan. When the program is coded it will also be natural to write this phrase as a comment immediately in front of the leading CONTINUE statement with its accompanying statement number.

The logical IF is suggested as the *only* method of realising a decision process which needs to be used. There are several other decision making instructions in Fortran which reflect an earlier stage of program language design and are best left alone. The logical IF itself has problems in use which stem from the necessity to present to any current computing system a single ordered sequence of consecutive statements even when a decision process is much more naturally presented as *two* sequences written side by side with one or the other being obeyed according as the decision is yes or no. Any one-dimensional rearrangement is sure to be lopsided since one of the alternative sequences must be written first, leaving the twin problems of how to relate the decision process to the second alternative and how to relate the end of the first alternative to that which should follow on directly but is now separated by the sequence representing the second alternative. We suggest the following arrangement be adopted as a standard

```
        IF( ) GO TO 22
C       ANSWER NO
        _____
        _____

        GO TO 33
C       ANSWER YES
     22 CONTINUE
        _____

C       END OF DECISION SEQUENCE
     33 CONTINUE
        _____
```

and that attempts to get the YES sequence to follow immediately on the logical IF by inverting the logical expression contained in the IF should be abandoned since they obscure the original meaning of the code. If the decision process is represented as a simple question at a higher level in the program plan with the alternative sequences labelled YES and NO (rather than "IF———" which implies that the YES sequence will come first), then the NO sequence can be written first to provide compatibility with the corresponding Fortran code. The special case where the YES sequence is just one instruction and the NO sequence is empty can of course be realized in the most natural manner.

```
        IF( ) YES statement
        next statement following decision
```

The programmer is warned against the use of too-complicated logical expressions in the logical IF. This probably indicates that the decision process implied is more clearly (and efficiently) realized as a hierarchy of decisions involving a *sequence* of logical IF's.

Again, the GO TO statement, as the most primitive method of breaking out of normal sequence generates many problems in practical use. A large number of GO TOs indicates that there are many strongly inter-related sections of code which are separated from each other in the program as it has been written down. This indicates that the decision processes in the program are very complicated and so it may be a good thing to check whether they can be simplified and co-ordinated to produce a smoother flow. If we have used CONTINUE statements as recommended previously then a more relevant criteria than counting GO TOs will be to have as few CONTINUEs as possible. Too many separate blocks of code prefaced by CONTINUE usually indicate that a large number of decision processes have been added as 'after-thoughts' to the program plan at a rather low level, typically as answers to the too-often repeated "Ah, yes – but what happens if the data is so-and-so: I hadn't thought of that". A restructuring of the program plan at a higher level and a consequent simplifying rearrangement at a lower level, producing fewer and longer CONTINUE blocks of sequential code, could well produce a more reliable program.

The STOP statement which is used to halt the execution of the program does not produce any organizational problems.

The DO statement, which appears the most natural way of specifying repetition provides many potential pitfalls. Most of these are concerned with determining how and when the repetition should end and arise from what appear to be useful generalizations. If we have, for example

```
        DO 22 I=J,K
```

where J and K are variables rather than fixed constants, then it is possible that K will be less than that of J when the statement is executed. How many times should the repetition be carried out? Some compilers do it once in any case, others do it not at all and may or may not warn the user that any special situation has occurred. The possible solution is to precede a DO statement of this type with a test for the special situation and a prevention of execution if it is not to be expected.

Another problem concerns the use of the value of the index variable (I in the previous example) after the repetition has been completed normally. This may or may not be equal to the value of K according to how and when the test to determine whether to repeat again is carried out in the compiled machine code, which depends on the compiler writer. Our preferred solution to both the problems is to avoid them completely. We recommend that *both* limits to the value of the index variable are always constants and that the *normal* completion of the repetition is specified explicitly by a logical IF inside the loop such as in the following pattern:

```
      DO 22 I=1,499
      _____
      _____
      IF(   )GO TO 33
      _____
      _____
   22 CONTINUE
      (report that repetition has occurred too many times)
      STOP
   33 CONTINUE
      (normal continuation of program)
      _____
      _____
```

In most real-world programs the conclusion of the repetition depends on some (expected) property of the data rather than on the value of an index, and the logical IF will reflect that properly. If by some chance, the data does not have that property, it is good to know that the program will stop of its own accord and not waste valuable resources in meaningless repetition. An even more radical solution to the problems of DO loops may be to dispense with them and use the more primitive but much more precise and well defined methods already introduced in chapter 8. This enables us to model precisely the several possible ways of specifying the completion of repetition, such as "repeat *until* a certain situation is true" or "repeat *while* a certain situation is true". It also enables us to count up or down an index value in any way we like as we repeat the sequence.

CALL and RETURN do not require further addition or comment except to reiterate the advice concerning the use of parameters rather than COMMON and as few of them as possible.

Input and output

Fortran provides a wealth of facilities surrounding input and output. Concerning executive statements, we would recommend that the familiar READ and WRITE are used exclusively, with no additional complications to those already introduced. Concerning the FORMAT statement, it is useful to introduce two new format specifiers, E and A, to add to I, F, X and H. E is used for reading or writing large values and enables them to be represented in something like the familar exponent form, such as "point two four five times ten to the fifth". If Y has the value 6.1745389, then

```
      WRITE(6,33)Y
      FORMAT(1X,E10.4)
```

will result in

(blank).6175E+01

The number after E gives the field width and the number after the decimal point in the FORMAT gives the number of figures behind the decimal point in the result. This is always followed by E and the sign and value of the exponent, generally two digits, or three if the number is very large or small and the size of storage locations in the particular computer permits it. Notice that the field width must be at least six to provide a significant figure in front of the E and that the result is rounded.

A value arranged as the previous output can be read in with a similar FORMAT statement. It is possible to miss out various parts of the input if these can be implied (such as missing out E and exponent value implies 'times ten to the power zero' that is the number as it stands) but this is not recommended.

The A format specification is specifically connected with the processing of characters and will be covered in the final section of this chapter.

Program structure

In this section we have the markers for the beginnings and ends of programs and subprograms. SUBROUTINE and END form a pair and the END statement also indicates the last statement of a main program. However, we do not have a first statement for the main program in the

existing standard Fortran. This is clearly an anomalous situation and compiler writers
often provide a main program starting line which carries as 'parameters' information about
the input files of data and output files of results. This may be standardized in the
future but for the present it will be necessary to consult the reference manuals for each
particular compiler and operating system which is being used.

Two other types of subprogram exist also in Fortran. It is possible to create a subprogram which can be activated like a library function, that is, by using its name with
relevant parameter values in an arithmetic expression. For example, the function PHI may
be defined in a subprogram as follows:

```
FUNCTION PHI(A)
PHI=A+A**2+B**3
RETURN
END
```

The parameter, in this case A, is used to provide values to the FUNCTION subprogram in the
same way as in a SUBROUTINE subprogram. However, parameters are *not* used to return a
result to the program which is making use of the function. Instead, a *single* value is
assigned to the *name* of the function, which for this purpose is treated as a simple variable
and it is this value which is returned when the name of the function is quoted in the program which requires it, in a statement such as

```
Z=Y+PHI(X)
```

The function name is associated with a value and so it must be of integer or real type.
This may be defined implicitly, using the Fortran naming convention, as we have already
shown, or explicitly, defined at the head of the using program by a statement such as

```
INTEGER RHO
```

and in the subprogram as, for example

```
INTEGER FUNCTION RHO
```

We recommend that FUNCTION subprograms should be limited to supplementing the standard
library functions where they do not provide a function which is often required by a
particular program. In the past programmers have tried to generalize the FUNCTION subprogram concept by such devious means as returning multiple results through the use of
COMMON arrays, that is, by producing *side effects* in a subprogram different from the
FUNCTION subprogram itself. This approach is now known to be incompatible with the
production of reliable programs.

The example we have provided produces a value for PHI through a single assignment statement with a single parameter. It is possible to have more than one input parameter and any
number of statements can be involved in producing a value for (in this case) PHI.

The older type of 'subprogram' is an even more restricted one defined by a single arithmetic assignment statement and comes from an earlier phase of language development. It can
be ignored.

Concerning the use of SUBROUTINE, it is possible to have as a parameter in addition to
constant and variable, the name of another subroutine. Considering the stress placed here
on the subroutine as an agent for imposing structure on a program rather than for saving
space by avoiding the duplication of pieces of similar code, it is clear that allowing for
such a wide variation in the fundamental actions of a specified subroutine is likely to be
counterproductive, and so this usage is not recommended.

Processing of characters

Finally, in this chapter we gather together certain features of Fortran which allow us to
do something entirely different to what has been possible before. This is concerned with
processing letters of the alphabet rather than numbers, and the relevant additional Fortran
features are an extension of the DATA statement and the A (for Alphabetic) specification in
the FORMAT statement.

In addition to a numerical value for a variable the DATA statement can provide an *alphabetical* value. For example, the statement

```
DATA I/1HK/
```

results in placing the individual character K into the computer storage location corresponing to the variable name I. The 1H between the slash characters acts rather like the H specification in the FORMAT statement in indicating that what follows is Hollerith or alphabetic information and the number in front of the H indicates how many characters are involved. The number of separate characters which can be contained in a single storage location will depend on the particular computer concerned but we will sidestep this issue by only ever specifying one character per location. We can assume that the spare space in the location is filled up with 'blank' characters in a standard manner. Any of the characters permitted in Fortran, including full stops, arithmetic signs and numerical digits can be specified in this way. Notice that the result of

```
      DATA I/1H3/
```

and

```
      DATA J/3/
```

is totally different on most computers in that I and J will carry the very different representations of 'character' 3 and 'binary coded' 3 and so, for example (I.EQ.J) will have the value *false* or *no* rather than *true* or *yes*. So these two methods of representation should not be mixed. We will show how to convert between one and the other later.

The A specification in the FORMAT statement is used when transferring alphabetic characters between input/output and storage locations corresponding to variable names. The same effect as

```
      DATA I/1HK/
```

can be produced by reading the 'value' K from an input data record as follows

```
      READ(5,22)I
   22 FORMAT(A1)
```

The A in the format shows that characters are being transferred and the 1 shows that there is one of them. I will then be given the value 'K' if that is what is in the first position of the input record. To write out the contents of I we can put

```
      WRITE(6,33)I
   33 FORMAT(1X,A1)
```

Character type data can be placed in an array. For example, we may place the characters from eighty positions of an input record into an 80-position array as follows:

```
      DIMENSION M(80)
      READ(5,22)(M(I),I=1,80)
   22 FORMAT(80A1)
```

Each location M(1), M(2), ...M(80) now contains *one* of the characters. Notice that we may choose to assign a character *value* to a variable which, by chance, coincides with its (single character) *name*

```
      DATA I/1HI/
```

There is *no* logical connection between the name I and the value 'I'. Notice also that there is a fundamental difference between A and H format specifications. A is *always* associated with a particular variable name while H *never* is. Character-type information can be associated with either integer or real names but difficulties can arise if both are used and we have elected to use only integer-type.

Once a variable has received a character-type value it can be specified in various other statements, in particular, assignment statements and logical IFs. For example:

```
      DATA I/1HK/
      N=I
```

results in both variables N and I having the value 'K': and we can then write statements like

```
      IF(I.EQ.N)GO TO 22
```

This implies that the variable I, having the value K is to be compared with the variable N,

which happens to have this value also and so the relational expression is *true*. It is
practical to use only the identity relation .EQ. and its inverse .NE. in this context and
both variables mentioned must have character-type values. The other relational operators
.GT. etc. will involve results which depend on the method of representing the characters in
a particular machine and detract from the portability of programs. If it is required to
sort characters into some sort of order it is better to convert each character into a
corresponding small integer value on input and sort the resulting numbers arithmetically,
converting back to the character form on output. In a similar way sequences of characters
representing *words* can be mapped into arithmetic equivalents and sorted. Here we can cover
only the direct processing of characters, where it is irrelevant to write such as

```
      M=I+N
```

where either or both of I and N have character values. It is remarkable that the very
limited facilities introduced have a wealth of application.

Let us assume that a data input record contains YES in the first three positions. Let
us read these characters into the first three locations of an array M with the statements

```
      DIMENSION M(10)
      READ(5,22)(M(I),I=1,3)
   22 FORMAT(3A1)
```

Then M(1), M(2) and M(3) will contain Y, E and S respectively. We can check for this by
adding the statements

```
      DIMENSION K(3)
      DATA K(1)/1HY/
      DATA K(2)/1HE/
      DATA K(3)/1HS/
```

at the head of the program and testing by the following sequence:

```
      DO 33 I=1,3
      IF(M(I).NE.K(I))GO TO 44
   33 CONTINUE
      _____
      _____

   44 CONTINUE
      _____
```

This successively tests M(1) and K(1), M(2) and K(2) and M(3) and K(3) for inequality. If
they are all equal (that is, the tests all *fail*) then the DO statement terminates normally
and we reach the statement *below*

```
   33 CONTINUE
```

This corresponds to the situation that Y, E and S *are* the values of M(1), M(2) and M(3),
that is, the letters YES occur as the first three characters of the input record. If we
reach

```
   44 CONTINUE
```

by means of a transfer from the logical IF, this means that the first three characters of
the input record are *not* Y E and S. This is the fundamental method of comparing two
sequences of characters for equality or inequality and is the only form of character *computation* necessary. The general principle is to set up a *known* test sequence in the program
with DATA statements and to test an *unknown* sequence for equality. Sequences of characters
of this type are generally called *strings*.

Sometimes a particular character sequence or string may be in the input record but it may
not occur as the *first* n characters because there are an indeterminate number of blank
characters in front of it. To detect this we may construct a *blank remover* as follows:

```
      DIMENSION M(10),K(3)
      DATA K(1)/1HY/
      DATA K(2)/1HE/
      DATA K(3)/1HS/
      DATA IBLANK/1H /
      READ(5,22)(M(I),I=1,10)
   22 FORMAT(10A1)
      DO 44 I=1,10                          ⎤
      J=I                                   ⎥  Blank
      IF(M(I).NE.IBLANK)GO TO 55            ⎥  remover
   44 CONTINUE                              ⎦
      (report that input line has been processed)
   55 CONTINUE
      DO 33 I=1,3                           ⎤
      N=J+I-1                               ⎥  YES
      IF(M(N).NE.K(I))GO TO 66              ⎥  recognizer
   33 CONTINUE                              ⎦
      (here report YES is recognized)
      GO TO 77
   66 CONTINUE
      (here report YES is not recognized)
   77 CONTINUE
```

This program reads the input record and processes it a character at a time from left to right. While there are leading blanks on the input record it moves through them until it reaches a non-blank character. At this point it transfers control to a character string recognizer, in this example for the string YES. For clarity, we have omitted tests which ensure the recognizer does not run off the end of the input array. Notice that the statement

```
      DATA IBLANK/1H /
```

which puts as the value of IBLANK the 'blank' character, is probably the most used statement in character processing, due to the use of blanks as separators between different strings of characters or words in natural language and other texts.

We need one further technique before a wide range of new processing is possible. This involves the conversion of numerical digits, read in as characters, into the equivalent numerical values which are useable in ordinary arithmetic. Let us consider the conversion of a single digit first.

First we read in the unknown digit from the input record with

```
      INTEGER DIGIT
      READ(5,22)DIGIT
   22 FORMAT(A1)
```

This digit may be any one of 1, 2, 3, ...9, 0. Let us require to put the numerical equivalent of this digit in IVALUE. We require to set up in the program the set of characters 1, 2, 3, ... 9, 0 to compare with the unknown input. We may do this by means of statements at the head of the program such as:

```
      DIMENSION NUMBER(10)
      DATA NUMBER(1)/1H1/
      DATA NUMBER(2)/1H2/

      DATA NUMBER(10)/1H0/
```

or by reading in the ten characters from an input record with

```
      DIMENSION NUMBER(10)               (at head of program)
      READ(5,23)(NUMBER(I),I=1,10)
   23 FORMAT(10A1)
```

The relevant integer value may then be placed in IVALUE by means of the sequence

```
      IVALUE=0
      IF(DIGIT.EQ.NUMBER(10))GO TO 44
      DO 33 I=1,9
      IF(DIGIT.NE.NUMBER(I))GO TO 33
      IVALUE=I
      GO TO 44
   33 CONTINUE
      CALL ERROR
   44 CONTINUE
```

We first set IVALUE to zero assuming that the value of DIGIT is '0' and then modify IVALUE if DIGIT is in fact any one of '1', '2', ... or '9'. If the DO statement is satisfied normally, then DIGIT does not contain one of 0, 1, ... 9 and therefore we transfer control to an error routine. After statement 44 we can make use of IVALUE as an ordinary integer. Notice the very messy way we have had to deal with the value zero. An alternative method involves putting '0' in NUMBER(1), '1' in NUMBER(2) etc., but we don't like that very much either. The difficulty arises from being unable to write NUMBER(0) in the Fortran language.

The conversion process is easily set up as a subroutine which we will make use of in the next section

```
      SUBROUTINE DIGIT(INPUT,INDEX,IVALUE)
      DIMENSION INPUT(80)
      DATA NUMBER(1)/1H1/

      DATA NUMBER(9)/1H9/
      DATA NUMBER(10)/1H0/
      IVALUE=0
      IF(INPUT(INDEX).EQ.NUMBER(10))RETURN
      DO 22 I=1,9
      IF(INPUT(INDEX).NE.NUMBER(I))GO TO 22
      IVALUE=I
      RETURN
   22 CONTINUE
      CALL ERROR
      END
```

Instead of testing a single variable DIGIT as previously we test and convert a single digit which occurs in any member of the input record array INPUT as defined by the current value of INDEX. The equivalent numerical value is returned by the third parameter, IVALUE. Subroutine ERROR does something about finding a character which is not a numerical digit.

Finally, we give a brief sketch of a program fragment which enables us to provide data input records in *free format*, that is, we are not tied to placing the data values in precise positions on the input record as dictated by a FORMAT statement in the program. The program also permits us to associated names with particular values on the input record. Both of these features *humanize* the input, in the sense that they make the input record easier to prepare and more readable for checking purposes. We would recommend this approach on all future programs.

The object of the program fragment is to process input records containing two possible two-letter codes (representing a chemical element or whatever we wish) followed by several digits representing an integer value. The two-letter code can have an arbitrary number of blanks in front of it and can be separated from the integer number by any number of blanks. The only positional requirement is that the two-letter code comes before the number.

```
      INTEGER INPUT(80),BLANK,C,U,Z
      DATA BLANK/1H /
      DATA C/1HC/
      DATA U/1HU/                              SAMPLE INPUT DATA
      DATA Z/1HZ/
      DATA N/1HN/                                 CU   35

      READ(5,32)(INPUT(I),I=1,80)            ] OBTAIN DATA
   32 FORMAT(80A1)

      INDEX=1

   22 CONTINUE
      IF(INPUT(INDEX).NE.BLANK)GO TO 33        BLANK IGNORER
      INDEX=INDEX+1
      IF(INDEX.GT.78)GO TO 77                  END OF CARD CHECK
      GO TO 22

   33 CONTINUE
      IF(INPUT(INDEX).NE.C)GO TO 44            COPPER
      IF(INPUT(INDEX+1).NE.U)CALL ERROR        RECOGNISER

      INDEX=INDEX+2

      CALL CHANGE(INPUT,INDEX,IVALUE)          COPPER VALUE
      CALL COPPER(IVALUE)                      PROCESSOR
      GO TO 66

   44 CONTINUE

      IF(INPUT(INDEX).NE.Z)CALL ERROR          ZINC
      IF(INPUT(INDEX+1).NE.N)CALL ERROR        RECOGNIZER

      INDEX=INDEX+2

      CALL CHANGE(INPUT,INDEX,IVALUE)          ZINC VALUE
      CALL ZINC(IVALUE)                        PROCESSOR

   66 CONTINUE
      ----------
                                               REST OF PROGRAM
      ----------
   77 CONTINUE
```

The calls to COPPER and ZINC do something appropriate with the relevant IVALUE. At statement 77 we do something about encountering the end of an input record.

```
      SUBROUTINE CHANGE(INPUT,INDEX,ITOTAL)
      DIMENSION INPUT(80)
      DATA IBLANK/1H /

      ITOTAL=0

   22 CONTINUE
      IF(INPUT(INDEX)NE.IBLANK)GO TO 33        BLANK
      INDEX=INDEX+1                            IGNORER
      IF(INDEX.GT.78)GO TO 44
      GO TO 22

   33 CONTINUE
      CALL DIGIT(INPUT,INDEX,IVAL)             BUILDING UP
      ITOTAL=ITOTAL*10+IVAL                    VALUE
      INDEX=INDEX+1
      IF(INDEX.GT.78)GO TO 44
      IF(INPUT(INDEX).NE.IBLANK)GO TO 33
      RETURN

   44 CONTINUE
      END
```

Subroutine CHANGE searches an array INPUT, starting at the initial value of INDEX, until it encounters a sequence of digits. It converts this sequence from individual characters in A1 format to an equivalent single integer value ITOTAL. On return from the call, INDEX carries the value corresponding to the space following the digit. At statement 44 we do something about encountering the end of the array INPUT.

The reader is advised to investigate the operation of this program fragment in detail, by inventing some sample input records and 'processing' them through simulating the program's operation by hand as described at the end of the previous chapter. This will provide practice also in reading a fairly complex program and there will no doubt be opportunities for correcting and improvement. Suitable error checks can be added (for example, what happens if the input record is completely blank or a value appears right at the end of the input record?) and the completed routines will provide a valuable contribution to the reader's collection of *software tools* for incorporation in future programs.

14 Further progress

So far, we have tried to present some basic principles of programming and to provide a practical introduction to a programming language. When the programming exercises have been completed, the reader should be in a position to make progress in several areas.

The first is in the preparation of programs which satisfy a practical requirement. It will be a surprise to discover how *large* a program is necessary to do something useful when all the features suggested in chapter 12 are incorporated and it will be a surprise how *long* it takes to produce. The reader is assured that these are facts of life and not a reflection of incompetence. If attempts are made to cut corners by glossing over the analysis and design stages it will be found that the projected point at which useful results are expected will move further away rather than closer and the time to completion may develop a Hartree constant, that is, always remain a fixed time ahead of 'now'.

The best way to gain experience is by the construction of programs which are *needed*. For this reason we have not provided here more programming problems than are necessary to establish the particular language features being explained. The selection of examples for practice will depend very much on the users area of interest and may be most usefully combined with studies of relevant techniques in a particular discipline. Examples of suitable texts are

    Jennings, A.   *Matrix Computation for Engineers and Scientists*
                   John Wiley and Sons, 1977

    Chambers, J.M. *Computational Methods for Data Analysis*
                   John Wiley and Sons, 1977

    La Fara, R.L. *Computer Methods for Science and Engineering*
                  {Hayden Book Co. U.S.A., 1973
                  {International Textbook Co. U.K., 1973

    Coats, R.B. and Parkin, A.   *Computer Models in the Social Sciences*
                   Edward Arnold, 1977

The second area for progress concerns the development of *software tools*. These are assemblies of subprograms and program fragments which do generally useful things in the user's area of interest. They are also practical equivalents of the user's mental building blocks, corresponding to higher level structures in the program plan. An important group of tools are those for setting up and processing data structures which are more complicated than the single variables and rectangular arrays inherent in Fortran. A comprehensive survey of such tools is provided in

    Naur, P.   *Concise Survey of Computer Methods*
            Petrocelli/Charter, 1974

which contains many Fortran examples. A key book for the would-be professional programmer is

    Kernighan, B.W. and Plauger, P.J.   *Software Tools*
                                   Addison Wesley Publishing Co., 1976

which stresses an organized approach to design from a totally practical viewpoint and provides a wealth of examples of more advanced tools. A book which contains many important ideas of making programs more useable is

    Gilb, T. and Weinberg, G.M.   *Humanized Input*
                       Winthrop Publishers, Cambridge, Mass., 1977

while innumerable ideas for improving detailed programming technique are available in

    Kernighan, B.W. and Plauger, P.J.   *The Elements of Programming Style*
                                   McGraw Hill Book Company, 1974

The third area for development is concerned with design methods and the management of programming projects to achieve results with the minimum of resources. An explanation of most of the important ideas in this area can be found in

    Myers, G.J.   *Software Reliability*
                  John Wiley and Sons, 1976

It will be up to the reader to look critically at these ideas, to experiment with them and to select those which prove genuinely useful. There are a large number of discussions in the literature which attempt to simplify the design process to following slavishly a series of simple rules and procedures. Many writers have even convinced themselves that such rules work for them in all circumstances. Certainly a series of conventions and habits can save time and thought, but as we have already emphasized, the problem solving process is inherently personal and psychological not objective and logical and so the choice of a method must remain a personal one.

Finally, we suggest a front on which progress is *not* necessary. Many new programmers assume that advanced programming means use of advanced and esoteric facilities in the programming language. It should be abundantly clear that our policy is to use the minimum of language facilities and especially to avoid the use of non-standard Fortran. The book

    Day, A.C.   *Compatible Fortran*
              Cambridge University Press, 1978

provides a carefully argued case for a minimum subset and can be used as a reference for our recommended version of Fortran. In order to discover the particular requirements of the local computer system it may be necessary to consult the relevant manufacturer's handbook. It is suggested that the new Fortran standard does not provide any new features which are so significant as to justify writing programs which are incompatible with existing compilers, and so this book summarizes the latest standard

    American National Standard Fortran (ANS X3J3/76, in draft)
         American National Standards Institute, Inc.

as well as the earlier

    American National Standard Fortran (ANS X3.9-1966)
        American National Standards Institute, Inc., 1966

If the user finds the language restrictive, we recommend the investigation of precompiler systems which interpret from an 'improved' language into standard Fortran and so avoid the use of a special full compiler and subsequent problems of maintenance. Such a system is used in the book 'Software Tools' by Kernighan and Plauger, referenced earlier.

The experienced user/programmer will always be searching for ways of *avoiding* programming. While we are a long way from the provision of a simple and obvious interface between user and computing system which can remove many of the difficulties of programming, it is now possible to call on program libraries and packages to provide ready built programs and subprograms to satisfy a variety of needs. The reader is advised to become thoroughly familiar with the range available on the local computer facility and to be aware how much time and effort can be saved with their use.

We are very much aware that our discussion of programming technique has taken place against the background of a computing system which carries out batch processing, that is monolithic programs of considerable size are processed as single entities and a block of 'results' is produced. The existence of networks of interactive terminals makes it possible to look forward to a more flexible method of developing solutions to problems essentially by involving the computing system in assisting with what are at present higher, less well defined levels of the program plan. At present though, computer terminals are used mainly as a convenient means of providing conventional programs for conventional operating systems. The methods described here are likely to be useful for some time.

Solutions to exercises

Many of the set exercises have more than one 'correct' solution. The solutions which follow are only suggested answers and we make no claim that they are the best.

Exercise 2

2.1   Read in the first number and call it SUM

> Read in the next number and call it NEXT
> Add NEXT to SUM to form the new SUM

Repeat the previous two instructions until there are no more numbers to process
Print out SUM
Stop

2.2
> Read in a NUMBER
> Compare NUMBER with VALUE
> If NUMBER is bigger, then add one to COUNT

Repeat the previous three instructions M-1 times
Print out COUNT
Stop

2.3
Read in a NUMBER

Repeat the previous instruction N times
Retrieve the FIRST number
Call it BIGGEST

> Retrieve the NEXT number
> Compare NEXT with BIGGEST
> If NEXT is larger, then BIGGEST is NEXT

Repeat until each member of the list has been compared

> Place BIGGEST at the top of the sorted list
> Go back and retrieve the NEXT number still left in
> the unsorted list
> Call NEXT the BIGGEST
> Retrieve NEXT number
> Compare and replace *as above*

Repeat the sequence until the whole list has been sorted
Print out sorted list
Stop

Exercise 3

3.1   (2.1) *Sum of positive numbers*

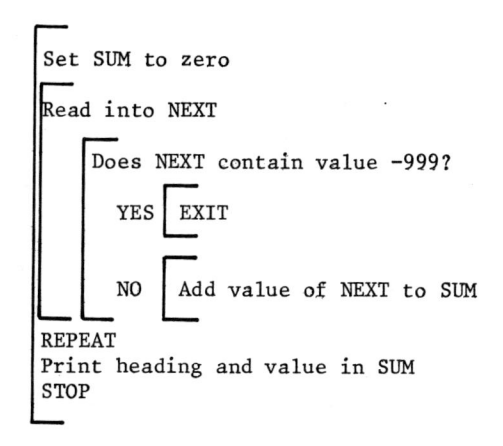

```
┌ Set SUM to zero
│ ┌ Read into NEXT
│ │   ┌ Does NEXT contain value -999?
│ │   │   YES ┌ EXIT
│ │   │       └
│ │   │
│ │   │   NO  ┌ Add value of NEXT to SUM
│ │   │       └
│ │   └
│ └ REPEAT
│ Print heading and value in SUM
│ STOP
└
```

(2.2) *Elements of a list greater than a given value*

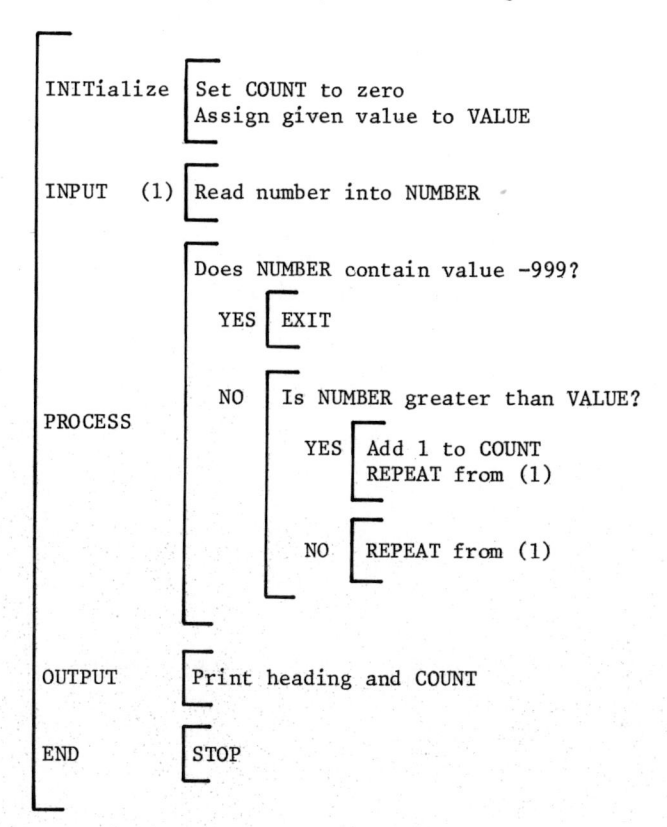

```
┌ INITialize  ┌ Set COUNT to zero
│             │ Assign given value to VALUE
│             └
│
│ INPUT  (1)  ┌ Read number into NUMBER
│             └
│             ┌ Does NUMBER contain value -999?
│             │   YES ┌ EXIT
│             │       └
│             │
│ PROCESS     │   NO  ┌ Is NUMBER greater than VALUE?
│             │       │   YES ┌ Add 1 to COUNT
│             │       │       │ REPEAT from (1)
│             │       │       └
│             │       │
│             │       │   NO  ┌ REPEAT from (1)
│             │       │       └
│             │       └
│             └
│
│ OUTPUT      ┌ Print heading and COUNT
│             └
│
│ END         ┌ STOP
│             └
└
```

Note the use of the device "REPEAT from (n)", where n marks a certain position in the program plan.
   Although most program plans can be arranged in a way which uses only "REPEAT"s (as in the first example), the above method often proves to be *clearer* in more complicated programs.

(2.3) *Sort program*

The solution offered for Exercise 2.3 is not entirely satisfactory although it probably satisfies the terms of the question: "Prepare outline solutions in rough note form". It leaves too many ends untied. How many times do you sort? How do you place a number at the top of a list? How do you miss out the numbers that have already been sorted? And so on. Some of these questions are more easily answered when you have an understanding of how the computer stores information and how the features provided by the programming language enable you to retrieve information, use it again and again, and to know how to keep a record of where everything is.

There are several methods of sorting. Here is one of them.

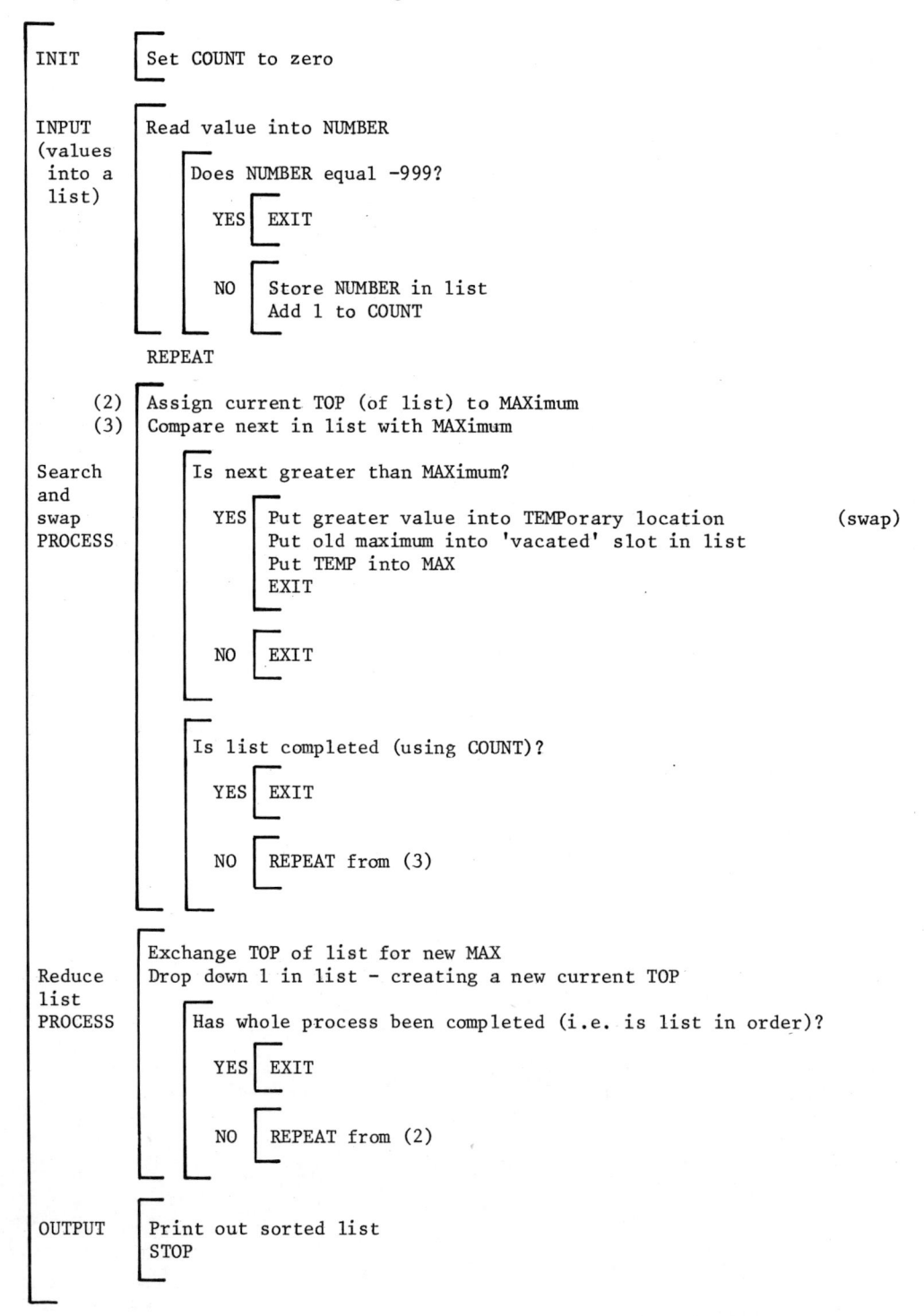

```
INIT            Set COUNT to zero

INPUT           Read value into NUMBER
(values
 into a             Does NUMBER equal -999?
 list)
                    YES  EXIT

                    NO   Store NUMBER in list
                         Add 1 to COUNT

                REPEAT

        (2)     Assign current TOP (of list) to MAXimum
        (3)     Compare next in list with MAXimum

Search          Is next greater than MAXimum?
and
swap                YES  Put greater value into TEMPorary location      (swap)
PROCESS                  Put old maximum into 'vacated' slot in list
                         Put TEMP into MAX
                         EXIT

                    NO   EXIT

                Is list completed (using COUNT)?

                    YES  EXIT

                    NO   REPEAT from (3)

                Exchange TOP of list for new MAX
Reduce          Drop down 1 in list - creating a new current TOP
list
PROCESS             Has whole process been completed (i.e. is list in order)?

                    YES  EXIT

                    NO   REPEAT from (2)

OUTPUT          Print out sorted list
                STOP
```

3.2 If negative values are allowed into the list, the end of data test cannot itself be a negative number. The end of data test will therefore have to be reconsidered.

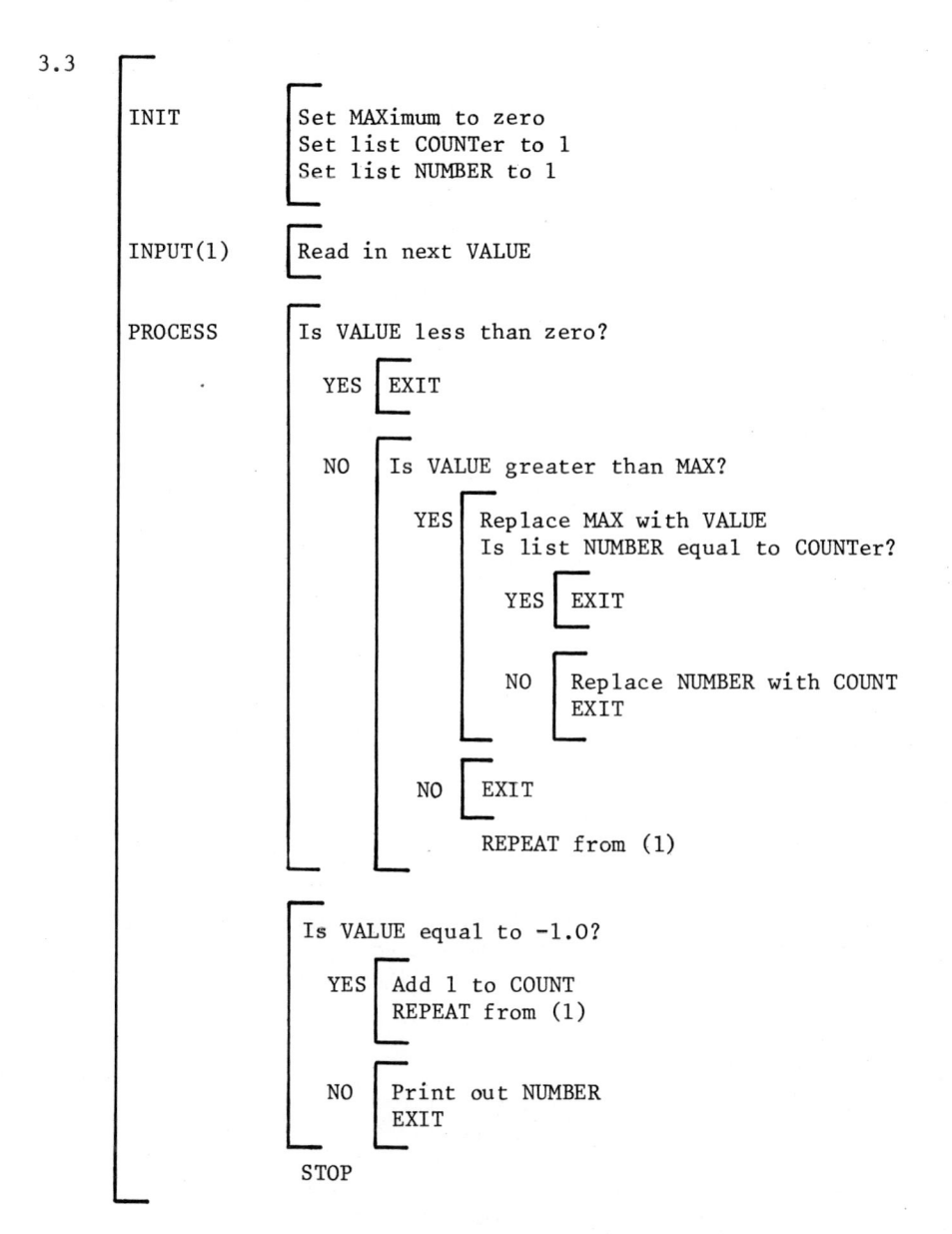

3.3
```
    ┌
    │ INIT         ┌ Set MAXimum to zero
    │              │ Set list COUNTer to 1
    │              │ Set list NUMBER to 1
    │              └
    │
    │ INPUT(1)     ┌ Read in next VALUE
    │              └
    │
    │ PROCESS      ┌ Is VALUE less than zero?
    │              │
    │              │    YES  ┌ EXIT
    │              │         └
    │              │
    │              │    NO   │ Is VALUE greater than MAX?
    │              │         │
    │              │         │    YES  ┌ Replace MAX with VALUE
    │              │         │         │ Is list NUMBER equal to COUNTer?
    │              │         │         │
    │              │         │         │    YES  ┌ EXIT
    │              │         │         │         └
    │              │         │         │
    │              │         │         │    NO   ┌ Replace NUMBER with COUNT
    │              │         │         │         │ EXIT
    │              │         │         │         └
    │              │         │
    │              │         │    NO   ┌ EXIT
    │              │         │         └
    │              │         │
    │              │         REPEAT from (1)
    │              └
    │
    │              ┌ Is VALUE equal to -1.0?
    │              │
    │              │    YES  ┌ Add 1 to COUNT
    │              │         │ REPEAT from (1)
    │              │         └
    │              │
    │              │    NO   ┌ Print out NUMBER
    │              │         │ EXIT
    │              │         └
    │              STOP
    └
```

Exercise 4

4.1 (1) real   (7) real
     (2) integer   (8) invalid (two points)
     (3) invalid (0 not valid)   (9) integer
     (4) real (positive sign can be included) (10) real
     (5) invalid (commas not permitted)   (11) real (leading zero not essential)
     (6) integer (negative sign valid)   (12) invalid (commas)

4.2 (1) real   (7) integer
     (2) real   (8) invalid ('.' is an illegal character)
     (3) integer   (9) invalid (seven characters)
     (4) real (embedded blank allowed)   (10) real
     (5) invalid (1st character a digit)   (11) real
     (6) integer (blank ignored)   (12) integer

Exercise 5

5.1   READ(5,64) IVALUE, JVALUE
    64 FORMAT(I3, 3X, I3)

5.2 Columns
   1 to 6   are used to form a real number allowing for three decimal places which is stored in AVALUE (F6.3).
   7 to 9   are ignored (3X).
   10 to 19 are used to form a real number allowing for four decimal places which is stored in BVALUE (F10.4).
   20 to 21 are ignored (2X)
   22 to 28 are used to form a real number allowing for three decimal places which is stored in CVALUE (F7.3).

5.3 The example contains the following four errors:
   The point (period) between NEXT and NUMBER should be a comma.
   AX is a real variable but the format specifies an integer value (I4). They must match in type.
   Assuming NUMBER is preceded by a comma and therefore becomes valid, an error occurs because F7.2 is the specification of the value being read into an integer store. They must match in type.
   The closing parenthesis is missing in the FORMAT statement.

5.4   WRITE(6,1004)DIST, BRED, ICOUNT, FRACT
    1004 FORMAT(1X,F10.2,10X,F10.3,10X,I10,10X,F10.3)

5.5 The following line of output would be produced:

   bbbbb45bbbb22.3456bbbbb280bbbbb128.293bb...b

   where be represents a blank space.
   Note that only 45 is printed from the contents of M since the field specified is I2. For a similar reason, the last digit is lost from the contents of Y. Also note that the first 1X of the 6X is used to control where the line is printed (i.e. the next available line).

Exercise 6

6.1 (1) A-(B+C)
     (2) A*(B+C)
     (3) ARC/(6.0+CAL)
     (4) A/B+XN
     (5) (A*X+B)*X+C
     (6) A**X+2.0
     (7) (A+23.2)/(135.6*D)
     (8) A*10.0**30/(-B*C)

6.2 (1) valid
     (2) invalid (mixed type arithmetic)
     (3) valid
     (4) valid
     (5) invalid (A*(B+C)+D)
     (6) invalid (2K not a variable name)
     (7) valid
     (8) valid
     (9) invalid (expression left of '=')
     (10) invalid (mixed type arithmetic)

6.3   IX=X

6.4   RBOX=IBOX

6.5   REAL1=INT1
       REAL2=INT2
       TEMP=INT1/INT2
       RESULT=REAL1/REAL2-TEMP

Exercise 7

7.1 (1) P.GT.X   (4) C.LE.D
     (2) Y.GT.2.5   (5) K.GE.L2
     (3) I.EQ.J   (6) J.NE.99

7.2 (1) X is less than Y   (4) ED is greater than 10.0
     (2) AB does not equal C   (5) MAX is less than or equal to 196
     (3) X is greater than or equal to B   (6) M1 is equal to 999

7.3
```
      READ(5,65) X
   65 FORMAT(F6.1)
      Y=3.0
      IF(X.GT.2.5) Y=0.0
      WRITE(6,87) Y
   87 FORMAT(1X,F6.1)
```

7.4
```
        READ(5,1000) Y
   1000 FORMAT(F6.1)
        X=Y
        IF(Y.EQ.1.0) X=0.0
        IF(Y.GT.1.0) X=Y*Y
```

7.5
```
       K=0
    10 CONTINUE
       READ(5,74)I, J
       IF(I.EQ.1) K=K+1
       IF(J.NE.9)GO TO 10
       WRITE(6,245)K
       STOP
    74 FORMAT(I1,8X,I1)
   245 FORMAT(10X,I8)
       END
```

7.6
```
        READ(5,1001)X
   1001 FORMAT(F7.3)
        IX=X
        Y=IX
        IF(Y.EQ.X)GO TO 99
        YI=IX/2
        YR=Y/2.0
        Y=IX-1
        IF(YI.EQ.YR)Y=IX+2
     99 CONTINUE
        WRITE(6,2002)X,Y
   2002 FORMAT(1X,F7.3,2X,F7.3)
        STOP
        END
```

Exercise 8

8.1 (1) invalid (negative subscript)   (6) invalid (subscript name too long)
     (2) invalid (real number subscript)   (7) valid
     (3) valid   (8) valid
     (4) valid (blank allowed in array name)   (9) invalid (real variable subscript)
     (5) invalid (zero subscript)

8.2   STORE=ALIST(10)

8.3
```
      TEMP=A(4)
      A(4)=A(3)
      A(3)=TEMP
```

8.4
```
      C(I)=A(I)*B(I)
```

8.5
```
      DIMENSION AR(20,100)
      _____
      
      SUM=0.0
      J=1
   10 CONTINUE
      I=1
   30 CONTINUE
      SUM=SUM+AR(I,J)
      I=I+1
      IF(I.LE.20)GO TO 30
      J=J+1
      IF(J.LE.100)GO TO 10
      _____
```

8.6 Five substitution operations *only* are required. These are:
```
      SUB(1)=SUB(5)
      SUB(2)=SUB(5)
      SUB(5)=SUB(4)
      SUB(4)=SUB(3)
      SUB(3)=SUB(5)    note that this SUB(5) is not the same as the original SUB(5)
```

Exercise 9

9.1
```
          MAX=0
          DO 24 I=1,100
          READ(5,1500) NUMBER
     1500 FORMAT(I3)
          IF(NUMBER.EQ.999)GO TO 125
          IF(NUMBER.GT.MAX) MAX=NUMBER
       24 CONTINUE
      125 CONTINUE
          WRITE(6,2400) MAX
     2400 FORMAT(1X,I3)
          STOP
          END
```

9.2 Change the DO statement to
```
          DO 24 I=1,200
```

9.3
```
          I=2**9
          DO 18 N=10,20
          I=2*I
          WRITE(6,2001)I,N
     2001 FORMAT(1X,I10,2X,I2)
       18 CONTINUE
          STOP
          END
```

Exercise 10

10.1 The program consists of a main routine and three subroutines. The main routine is used solely to bring the subroutines into execution. Communication between the routines is established by using parameters.
The first CALL from the main routine is to SUBROUTINE IN using the parameters A, B and XY, which at the time of the CALL have had no values assigned to them.
On entry to IN, the dummy parameters AA, BB and XYXY refer to A, B and XY respectively. The subroutine is an input routine for reading values from a single data card, storing 9.6 in A, 1684.0 in B and 8.75Ø2 in XY. Following the RETURN from IN to the main routine a CALL is made to SUBROUTINE ARITH, using the parameters A, B, XY and EQU. At this stage EQU has no value, it is a variable set up to receive a value from SUBROUTINE ARITH.
On entry to ARITH, the dummy parameters A, B, XY and EQU refer to A, B, XY and EQU in the main routine. (It so happens in this instance that the names are the same). The subroutine evaluates an arithmetic expression involving A, XY and B, and assigns the result (1768.00192) to EQU (in the main routine) before the RETURN of control to the main routine.
The third and final CALL is to SUBROUTINE OUT using the argument EQU.
On entry to OUT, the dummy parameter EQU becomes equivalent to EQU in the main routine, and hence the result of the calculation performed by ARITH is passed to OUT which is responsible for printing out the result. The FORMAT specifies an F1Ø.2 field, hence only 1768.ØØ is printed out. Following the RETURN to the main routine, the STOP statement is executed and the program terminates.

Exercise 11

11.1
```
        DIMENSION A(1Ø)
        READ(5,12ØØ) (A(I),I=1,6)
   12ØØ FORMAT(6F1Ø.3)
```

11.2
```
        DO 25 I=1,1Ø
        WRITE(6,24ØØ) (AR(I,J),J=1,5)
   24ØØ FORMAT(1X,5F1Ø.4)
     25 CONTINUE
```

11.3 The value in A is printed in the first ten positions of the first line of a new page. There are four blank lines before the value in B is printed in the first ten positions of a new line.

11.4 The READ statement within the DO loop takes a single value from a data card each time the subscript K is incremented. 5 data cards are therefore required. Using the implied DO loop all 5 values are taken from *one* card.

11.5
```
        IF(X.GT.Y.AND.A.GT.C)
```

11.6
```
        DO 25 I=1,1Ø
        DO 25 J=I,1Ø
        IF(I.EQ.J)GO TO 25
   C
   C    NOT WORTH SWAPPING MAJOR DIAGONAL AS IS THE SAME POINT
   C
        TEMP=A(I,J)
        A(I,J)=A(J,I)
        A(J,I)=TEMP
     25 CONTINUE
```

11.7
```
          DIMENSION X(80)
    C   READ IN THE NUMBERS
          READ(5,1000)(X(I),I=1,80)
    C
    C  PLACE THEM IN ORDER
      240 CONTINUE
          K=0
          DO 75 I=1,79
          IF(X(I).GE.X(I+1))GO TO 350
          B=X(I)
          X(I)=X(I+1)
          X(I+1)=B
          K=K+1
      350 CONTINUE
       75 CONTINUE
          IF(K.NE.0)GO TO 240
    C
    C  PRINT OUT IN SEQUENCE
          DO 65 I=1,80
          WRITE(6,2000)X(I)
       65 CONTINUE
          STOP
    C
     1000 FORMAT(8F10.4)
     2000 FORMAT(10X,F10.4)
          END
```

Appendix 1 Control statements

An example of the job control instructions for running a simple Fortran job on the CDC computer system at Imperial College

The computer system must first recognize a number of key cards before it is able to accept and run a program. It must also find certain cards which act as separators or terminators within the card deck. Collectively these cards are referred to as job control cards or directives.

Control cards and deck order

1	JOB(aaaaaaa)	to identify the program as belonging to a recognized user
2	PASSWORD(bbbbbbb)	to substantiate the validity of the job number
3	MAP(P)	to request information which may help to isolate an error discovered during program execution
4	FORTRAN(T,D)	to call in the FORTRAN compiler to translate the program instructions which follow
5	7/8/9	to separate the control cards from the program instructions and called the *END OF RECORD* card
6	C	a card with the following information punched on it: programmer's name in columns 20 - 30 program number (1 to 5) - col. 35 programmer's group (groupn, where n is 1 to 12) col. 39 - 46
	BLOCK OF STATEMENTS FORMING THE FORTRAN PROGRAM	
7	7/8/9	to separate the program from the data (*END OF RECORD* card)
	BLOCK CONTAINING THE DATA FOR THE PROGRAM	
8	6/7/8/9	to mark the end of the program deck; that is the *final* card and called the *END OF FILE* card

On the JOB and PASSWORD cards aaaaaaa and bbbbbbb represent special 1 - 7 character identifications. The password is included to give the job number more security. The characters on the special marker cards (5, 7 and 8) are all punched in the first column.

The MAP card is not obligatory for general use. It is used here because of the useful information it can provide when certain errors occur in the program.

The comment card (6) is not a necessity for general use of the system but it is *essential* for identification purposes when different programmers are using the same job number.

Example program deck

```
JOB(aaaaaaa)
PASSWORD(bbbbbbb)
MAP(P)
FORTRAN(T,D)
```
END OF RECORD CARD
```
C                   JACKSON.P     2    GROUP 6
C   TEST PROGRAM TO READ TWO DATA CARDS
        READ(5,1100) NDAY, MONTH, NYEAR
   1100 FORMAT(3X,I2,3X,I2,1X,I4)
        READ(5,1150)TEMP
   1150 FORMAT(F5.2)
C    PRINT OUT DATA TO CHECK
        WRITE(6,2200) NDAY, MONTH, NYEAR, TEMP
   2200 FORMAT(1X,I2,1X,I2,1X,I4,10X,F5.2)
        STOP
        END
```
END OF RECORD CARD
```
    27   9 1978
18.25
```
END OF FILE CARD

Appendix 2   Number representation

The maximum or minimum magnitude of *real* and *integer* constants depends on the computer being used, as shown below:

Computer	Approximate Real		Integer
	maximum	minimum	Maximum
IBM 370	10^{75}	10^{-75}	$2^{31}-1$
ICL 1900	10^{76}	10^{-76}	$2^{23}-1$
ICL 2900	10^{75}	10^{-75}	$2^{31}-1$
CDC 6000	10^{322}	10^{-293}	$2^{47}-1$
CDC 7600	10^{322}	10^{-293}	$2^{47}-1$
UNIVAC 1110	10^{38}	10^{-38}	$2^{35}-1$

Imperial College's Cyber 174 and 6500 computers belong to the same CDC series as the 6000. By comparison it can be seen that the CDC machines are large 'number crunching' computers. However, it needs to be appreciated that for calculation and the printing of results the accuracy of a number does not exceed 14 significant figures.

The number of characters that can be printed out on a single line of output is a property of the lineprinter and varies with the equipment in use. 132 columns per line is generally quoted as the standard figure but the CDC printers accommodate 136 characters. On the Imperial College system, therefore, a WRITE statement cannot use a FORMAT statement which specifies a line of output of more than 136 characters.

Index

Accuracy 27-28, 91
Arithmetic 24-28
  expressions 25-27, 51-52
  operators 25
Arrays 36-39, 40, 42, 51-52
Assignment statement 24, 67

CALL statement 44-48, 51, 61
Characters 14
  character processing 71-77
Comment line 16
COMMON 50-51, 61, 65-67
  blank 67
  labelled 66
  unlabelled 67
Compilation 12
Constants 14
Continuation of a statement 15-16
CONTINUE statement 32-34, 40-42, 69-70
Control commands 13, 89-90

Data 1, 12, 14, 65-66
DATA statement 68, 71-76
Defensive programming 63
DIMENSION declaration 37-39, 42, 48, 65
DO statement 40-43, 52, 69
  problems with 69, 70
Documentation 64

End of file marker 13, 89-90
End of record marker 13, 89-90
END statement 21-22, 44-45, 70
Execution 12
Exercises
  2 6, 80
  3 10-11, 81-83
  4 16, 83
  5 22, 84
  6 28, 84
  7 34, 85
  8 39, 85-86
  9 43, 86
  10 49, 87
  11 56-57, 87-88
Explicit type declaration 65

Families of statements 65
Formats
  A 71-74, 76
  E 70
  F 19
  H 53
  I 17-18
  X 18
FORMAT statement 17-22

Fortran statement 15-16
FUNCTION statement 71
Functions, library 55-56, 67-68
  FLOAT 68
  IFIX 68
  SQRT 55

GO TO statement 30-34
  problems with 69

Hierarchy of operators 25, 55

IF, logical 30-34, 69
  logical expression 31-34, 54-55
  logical operators, AND, OR, NOT 54-55
Implicit type declaration 65
Implied DO 52
Integer arithmetic 26
  constant 14
  variable 15
INTEGER type declaration 66

Job control commands 89

Logical IF statement 30-34

Operating system 12

Parameter, in subroutines 45-48, 50-51
Printer control 20, 53-54
Problem analysis 58
Program 3, 7, 12-13, 21
Program construction 58
Program design 59
Program exercises
  1 23
  2 28
  3 35
  4 39, 43
  5 49
Program plan 6, 7-10, 60
Program qualities 58
  easy to use 59
  endurance 59
  efficiency 59
  maintainability 59
  modifiability 59
  modularity 59
  portability 59
  readability 61
  reliability 59
  robustness 59
  understandability 59
Programming language standards 64

READ statement   17-19, 40-41, 52
Real constant   14
  variable   15
REAL type declaration   66
Relational operators   31, 55
RETURN statement   45-47

Software tools   77
Standard Fortran   64
Statement numbers   15, 30, 61
STOP statement   21-22
String, definition of   73

SUBROUTINE statement   44-48, 51, 61
Subroutines   44-48, 50-51
Subscripted variables   36-39, 51
Successive refinement   60

Testing by hand   62

Variables   14-15, 61
  type   65

WRITE statement   19-21, 52-53
Writing conventions for coding forms   16